the
twelve days of

aga

christmas

Sarah Whitaker teaches Aga cooking. She is one of the small group of officially trained and approved Aga-Rayburn demonstrators, and regularly demonstrates throughout the UK in Aga and Rayburn showrooms and dealerships, as well as in private houses.

Sarah has compiled a book packed with quick and easy ideas, tips and techniques to make Christmas less of a marathon and to make your Aga work better for you throughout the year.

From her thatched cottage in a rural Hampshire village, Sarah specialises in Aga cookery demonstrations and writing delicious recipes. Her career has been interesting and varied: cooking in staff canteens, wine bars, city dining rooms and even a van in the middle of a field – feeding film crews, cabinet ministers and rock stars!

Sarah has appeared on Meridian TV and BBC radio, in the Aga Magazine, the Sunday Times, 'House Beautiful' magazine and the international cookery magazine 'Semana Cocina'. One of her wedding cakes even featured in 'Hello!' magazine.

Sarah is happy to demonstrate for you in her own kitchen or in yours – gather a group of friends and spend a morning learning the secrets of Aga cooking, just for fun or as a charity fundraising event.

the
twelve days of
aga
christmas

recipes collected by
sarah whitaker

First published 2003, reprinted 2004, 2005, 2006 (twice)
and 2007 (twice)

Published by Sarah Whitaker
The Trout, Nether Wallop, Stockbridge, Hampshire, SO20 8EW
www.sarahwhitaker.com

ISBN 978-0-9554306-1-9

Produced by Action Publishing Technology Ltd, Gloucester
Printed in Great Britain

contents

There is no such thing as an original recipe. If I have inadvertently duplicated anyone else's ideas, I apologise – sometimes I think there must be a spy in my kitchen when I see a television cook make a dish that I thought I had invented the day before!

Details of demonstrations, further copies of this book and copies of Sarah's other recipe collections:

'Home Made in Nether Wallop'

and

'Relaxed Aga Cooking'

are available from:

The Trout, Nether Wallop, Hampshire, SO20 8EW

e mail: sarah@sarahwhitaker.com

www.sarahwhitaker.com

getting to know your aga

Life with an Aga or range cooker is like a friendship. Its warm, benign presence in the kitchen is such a comfort in the house.

The Aga will cook any food you want, quickly or slowly, perfectly. From a slow-roasted Christmas turkey to a piece of toast, it is the ultimate cooker. For some people, it is the cast iron monster in the kitchen, frightening in the extreme – all those doors and no visible controls, where on earth do you start?

Put simply, an Aga has two top plates: the left hand *boiling plate,* which is very hot – it boils. The right hand, *simmering plate*, is about half the temperature of the boiling plate – it simmers. The two-oven Aga has a top, *roasting oven*, which is very hot – it roasts, and a lower, *simmering oven* that is about half the temperature of the roasting oven – it simmers. The three-oven Aga has an additional *baking oven* that runs at a perfect temperature for baking, about half way between the roasting and simmering ovens. The four-oven Aga also has a *warming oven*, cooler than the simmering oven. And that's it.

The Aga is a heat storage cooker, it maintains its heat until the lids are opened for too long or very cool food is put into the ovens, when the thermostat kicks in and the heat gradually regenerates. About 80% of all cooking on an Aga takes place in the oven, saving heat and fuel. This has the added benefit of no spitting fat to clear up and no cooking smells – the ovens are vented to the flue and all smells just disappear up the chimney.

All my Aga recipes refer to hanging the tins and shelves from the runners at the sides of the ovens. **Always count the runners downwards from the top of the oven**.

Always hot, always ready to cook, the Aga is an all-in-one cooker: you will no longer need an electric kettle, an electric toaster, a toasted sandwich maker, a rice steamer, a bread maker or a tumble dryer and it is a magnet for pets! I frequently have to clear away the drying washing and football kit, the dog and the drying-up before I start to cook.

the turkey!

In the Aga, cook the turkey in the simmering oven, long and slow – as a general rule, if you put it in at bedtime, it will be cooked by late elevenses! This leaves the roasting oven free for roasting the potatoes, sprouts and parsnips and grilling the sausages, bacon rolls etc.

To cook the turkey:

Place the turkey (upside down if you like!, on its breast), in the large roasting tin.

Stuff the neck cavity only – I tend to cook the stuffing separately, we have more than once forgotten that the stuffing was in the bird until too late! If not putting stuffing into the bird, peel and cut up an onion and push that into the cavities, with a little butter – leave the neck in the cavity to keep it moist without stuffing. *Weigh the turkey after it has been stuffed to calculate the cooking time.*

Smear the bird with some butter, then cover it tightly with foil around the edge of the tin.

Slow roasting the turkey:

The simmering oven runs at about half the temperature of the roasting oven, so the turkey will take twice as long to cook in it.

If your turkey weighs more than 16 lb (7kg), put it into the roasting oven for an hour, then transfer to the simmering oven overnight.

For turkeys under 16 lb (7kg), just put into the simmering oven and let the Aga do the rest!

All Agas cook at slightly different speeds, an older Aga will take a little longer than a new one, but as a rough guide:

8 – 10 lb (3 – 4$\frac{1}{2}$kg) turkeys will take about 8 – 10 hours
10 – 16 lb (4$\frac{1}{2}$ – 7kg) turkeys will take about 9 – 12 hours
16 – 22 lb (7 – 10kg) turkeys will take about 10 – 14 hours

Next day, check the turkey mid-morning, it should be almost cooked. Pierce the thigh with a skewer and if the juices run clear, it is cooked.

When you and the turkey are ready, remove the foil and turn the bird over (if it was cooked on its breast) and pour off the juices – *this is easiest if you have a second, clean roasting tin and just transfer the bird from one tin to the other, leaving the juices in the first*. Put the turkey into the roasting oven, uncovered, for up to half an hour to brown, while you make the gravy. Once the breast is browned, transfer to a serving plate and allow to rest for at least 15 minutes before carving.

If it is completely cooked at 11am and you plan to eat at 3pm, DON'T PANIC! Re-cover with the foil then lay a large bath towel, folded into quarters, or a cot duvet or your fleece jacket, or all three, over it and place it beside the Aga (on a 4 oven Aga, put it onto the warming plate on the top) and *just leave it*. It has taken about 12 hours to get really hot and cooked through; it won't cool down in any sort of hurry!

If it is not cooked through, re-cover and return it to the simmering oven. Check it again in an hour.

Fast roasting the turkey:

Put the foil-covered turkey into the roasting oven and cook it.

Timing:

8 – 10 lb (3 – 4½kg) turkeys will take about 2 hours
10 – 16 lb (4½ – 7kg) turkeys will take about 2½ to 3 hours
16 – 22 lb (7 – 10kg) turkeys will take about 3 to 3½ hours

Every family has its own idea of what constitutes the perfect Christmas dinner with all the trimmings – here are just a few ideas to choose from!

gravy

Serves 6 – 8

1 pint (550ml) turkey stock or giblet stock or stock mixed with wine or water and a stock cube
1 tbsp plain flour
1 tbsp turkey fat or the juices from the roasted bird
Salt and pepper

Oven:
Aga roasting oven, 400F, 200C, Gas 6

Prepare ahead:
24 hours

Freeze:
Yes

1. When the turkey has cooked, pour off the juices from the roasting tin. *This is easiest if you have a second, clean roasting tin and just transfer the bird from one tin to the other, leaving the juices in the first.* Cover the bird with foil and allow it to rest while you make the gravy and dish up all the vegetables.

2. Pour the juices into a jug, leaving a tablespoonful or two in the bottom of the pan. Stir in the flour, then gradually blend in the reserved stock and seasoning.

3. Put the tin onto the floor of the roasting oven to boil. Stir after about 5 minutes, then return to the oven for a further 5 minutes until boiling and thickened. Strain and serve.

easy peasy cheat's stuffing

Serves 6

A packet of ready made stuffing mix
2 oz (55g) butter
Grated rind of a lemon

Optional extra flavourings:
Chopped ready to eat apricots
Chopped walnuts

1. Mix according to the packet instructions then stir in the butter and lemon rind.

2. Add the apricots and/or walnuts then either stuff into the neck cavity of the turkey or pile into a greased ovenproof dish and bake in the roasting oven for 20 minutes.

sausage and chestnut stuffing

Serves 6 – 8

1 lb (450g) sausage meat
7 oz (200g) chestnuts
1 onion
1 tbsp olive oil
Salt and pepper
1 tbsp chopped parsley
1 tbsp chopped fresh tarragon
or marjoram

Oven:
Aga roasting oven, 400F, 200C,
Gas 6

Prepare ahead:
24 hours

Freeze:
Yes

1. Peel and chop the onion. Heat the oil and add the chopped onion. Cook for a minute until sizzling, then cover and transfer to the simmering oven for 15 minutes until softened.

2. Tip the sausage meat, chestnuts, onions, seasoning and herbs into a processor and whizz until mixed. Either stuff into the neck cavity of the turkey or turn out into a greased ovenproof dish and bake for 25 minutes.

prune and apricot stuffing

Serves 6 – 8

1 onion
1 clove garlic
1 tbsp olive oil
2 oz (55g) ready to eat prunes
2 oz (55g) ready to eat dried apricots
4 oz (110g) fresh breadcrumbs
1 egg
1 tbsp chopped fresh parsley
1 tbsp chopped fresh marjoram

Oven:
Aga roasting oven, 400F, 200C, Gas 6

Prepare ahead:
24 hours

Freeze:
Yes

1. Chop the onion and crush the garlic. Heat the oil and add the onion and garlic. Cook for a minute until sizzling, then cover and transfer to the simmering oven for 15 minutes until softened.

2. Chop the prunes and apricots and add to the pan, with the breadcrumbs, herbs and seasoning. Stir in enough beaten egg to bind the mixture.

3. Stuff into the neck cavity of the turkey or turn out into a greased ovenproof dish and bake for 25 minutes.

cranberry sauce

Makes 3 jars – one to eat on Christmas Day and two to give as presents!

1 lb (450g) cranberries
¼ oz (2g) root ginger, chopped
1 stick cinnamon, broken up
¼ oz (2g) whole allspice, bruised
6 cloves
½ pint (275ml) cider vinegar
8 oz (275g) demerara sugar

Oven:
Floor of roasting oven or hob of conventional cooker

Prepare ahead:
4 weeks

Freeze:
No

1. Put the spices and ginger into a muslin bag. Put into a large pan, with the cranberries, sugar and vinegar.

2. Slowly bring to the boil, then transfer to the floor of the roasting oven, uncovered for about 15 minutes, until soft and reduced.

3. Remove from the heat, take out the bag of spices and pour into warmed, sterilised jars. Seal the jars whilst still hot.

1. To sterilise the jars for cranberry sauce – or any other preserve – just wet some clean jam jars and put them into the simmering oven. When they are dry, they are sterile as the water has boiled off in the heat of the oven.

2. I usually put the jars into the oven in a roasting tin, so that they are all kept together and none can escape when you get them out to fill.

3. Keep the jars in the tin while you fill them, so that any overflows are contained in the tin and don't make your kitchen worktop all sticky!

4. Put a layer of cling film between the top of the jar and the metal lid, so that the vinegar does not corrode it over time.

bread sauce

Serves 6 – 8

1 pint (550ml) milk
1 onion
6 cloves
1 bay leaf
Blade of mace
Salt and pepper
5 slices day-old bread, crusts on or off according to taste!
½ oz (10g) butter

Oven:
Aga simmering oven, 250F, 130C, Gas 1

Prepare ahead:
24 hours, reheat in simmering oven for an hour

Freeze:
Yes

1. Peel the onion and chop it. Put it into a pan with the cloves, bay leaf, mace, seasoning and milk and slowly bring to the boil. Cover and put into the simmering oven for half an hour.

2. Whizz the bread to crumbs in a processor.

3. Strain the onion and flavourings from the milk, then stir in the breadcrumbs and allow to stand for 5 minutes, for the bread to soak into the milk.

4. Stir in the butter and serve.

roast potatoes

Serves 6 – 8

1 lb (450g) King Edward potatoes
1 oz (25g) goose fat, beef dripping or 1 tbsp olive oil
1 tbsp plain flour

Oven:
Aga roasting oven, 400F, 200C, Gas 6

Prepare ahead:
Yes, allow to cool then reheat for 5 minutes just before serving

Freeze:
YES!

1. If using dripping or goose fat, set in a bowl on the back of the Aga to melt.

2. Line the small shallow baking tray with Bake-O-Glide.

3. Peel the potatoes and cut into even sized pieces. Put into a pan of cold water. Cover, bring to the boil, and simmer for a minute. Drain then add the flour. Shake well, then pour in the fat and shake again.

4. Tip the coated potatoes into the tin and hang from the second set of runners and cook for about an hour, until crisp and golden.

Cooking the roast potatoes in a shallow dish makes them much crisper.

If you roast potatoes – or any vegtable – in a deep roasting tin, the sides of the tin protect the vegetables from the intense heat from the sides of the Aga oven, preventing them from cooking as fast; they almost steam as they roast, making them soggy instead of crisp.

fanned potatoes

Serves 6 – 8

4 baking potatoes
4 sweet potatoes
2 tbsp olive oil
Mixed dried herbs
Salt and pepper

Oven:
Aga roasting oven,
400F, 200C, Gas 6

Prepare ahead:
30 minutes

Freeze:
No

1. Wash the potatoes. Cut each one into thin (1/4"/ 1/2 cm) slices, holding the potato firmly to keep its shape.

2. Line a shallow baking tray with Bake-O-Glide.

3. Put the potatoes onto the tray then gently push them over, like a row of collapsed dominoes.

4. Spoon over the oil, sprinkle with herbs and seasoning.

5. Hang from the second runners and bake for an hour, until cooked through and golden.

stilton mash

Serves 4 – 5

1½ lb (600g) potatoes
¼ pint (150ml) creamy milk
1 oz (25g) butter
2 oz (50g) Stilton cheese
Salt and pepper
Grated nutmeg

Oven:
Aga simmering oven, 250F,
130C, Gas 1

Prepare ahead:
Will keep warm for up to an
hour

Freeze:
Yes

1. Set the milk and butter in a jug on the back of the Aga to warm.

2. Cut the potatoes into even sized pieces. Bring to the boil on the boiling plate, drain, cover and put into the simmering oven for about 30 minutes until soft.

3. Mash, then add the milk, butter, salt, pepper and a good grating of nutmeg, then crumble in the Stilton. Beat with a wooden spoon until smooth.

Variations for mashed potato:

1. Add a couple of tablespoons of grainy mustard to the mash instead of the Stilton.

2. Add a couple of tablespoons of sun-dried tomato paste to the mash instead of the Stilton – for a wonderfully bright orange-red mash!

3. Add some chopped spring onions to the mash for colcannon.

rosti cake

Serves 4

4 large potatoes
1 onion
6 rashers smoked back bacon
¼ pint (150ml) milk
1 tbsp plain flour
2 eggs
Salt and pepper

Oven:
Aga roasting oven, 400F, 200C, Gas 6

Prepare ahead:
1 hour

Freeze:
Yes

1. Cut the bacon into small dice. Heat an oven proof frying pan on the simmering plate and add the bacon. Cook until sizzling, then place on the floor of the roasting oven for 5 minutes, stirring occasionally, until the bacon is crisp. Tip the bacon into a bowl.

2. Peel the onion and grate into the bowl with the bacon. Grate in the potatoes. Stir in the flour, then the seasoning, egg and milk. Pour into the still-warm frying pan and put onto the floor of the roasting oven for 25 minutes then transfer to the top of the oven for a further 20 minutes, until brown and crispy on the bottom and golden on top.

honey and orange glazed carrots

Serves 4

1 lb (450g) carrots
2 oz (55g) butter
1 tsp runny honey
Grated rind of an orange
Salt and pepper
1 tbsp chopped parsley

Oven:
Aga simmering oven, 250F, 130C, Gas 1

Prepare ahead:
Yes, 1 hour cooked

Freeze:
Yes, cooked

1. Peel the carrots, cut into even sized pieces and put into a pan of cold water.
2. Cover, bring to the boil, drain then cover and put into the simmering oven for about 15 minutes until tender.
3. Return the pan to the simmering plate and add the butter, honey, orange rind and seasoning. Shake the pan then sprinkle with parsley and serve.

mashed parsnips and potatoes with stilton

Serves 4

8 oz (225g) parsnips
8 oz (225g) white potatoes
2 oz (55g) Stilton cheese
4 tbsp milk
1 oz (25g) butter
Salt and pepper

Oven:
Aga simmering oven, 250F, 130C, Gas 1

Prepare ahead:
I hour

Freeze:
Yes

1. Set the milk and butter in a jug on the back of the Aga to warm.
2. Cut the potatoes and parsnips into even sized pieces. Put into a pan and cover with water. Bring to the boil then drain, cover and put into the simmering oven for about 30 minutes until soft.
3. Crumble in the cheese and mash thoroughly with the milk, butter and seasoning.

parsnips mashed with sherry

Serves 4 – 6

1 lb (450g) parsnips
1 oz (25g) butter
2 tbsp medium sherry
Salt and pepper

Oven:
Aga simmering oven, 250F,
130C, Gas 1

Prepare ahead:
Yes

Freeze:
Yes

1. Cut the parsnips into even sized pieces. Put into a pan of cold water, bring to the boil, drain and put into the simmering oven for about 20 minutes until soft.

2. Mash thoroughly with the butter, salt, pepper and sherry.

celeriac and chestnut mash

Serves 6

1 bulb celeriac
7 oz (200g) pack prepared, vacuum packed chestnuts
2 tbsp fromage frais
1 oz (25g) butter
Sprig of thyme
1 bayleaf
Salt and pepper

Oven:
Aga simmering oven, 250F,
130C, Gas 1

Prepare ahead:
1 hour

Freeze:
Yes

1. Peel the celeriac and cut into even sized pieces. Put into a pan and cover with water. Bring to the boil then drain, cover, add the herbs and put into the simmering oven for 20 minutes.

2. Tip in the chestnuts, re-cover and return to the oven for a further 5 minutes. Remove the herbs and discard.

3. Stir in the butter and fromage frais then mash thoroughly. Add more fromage fr[a] the purée is too thick. Season well and serve.

roasted sprouts with chestnuts and bacon

Serves 4

1 lb (450g) sprouts
2 tbsp olive oil
Salt and pepper
4 oz (110g) bacon pieces
4 oz (110g) peeled and
prepared chestnuts

Oven:
Aga roasting oven, 400F, 200C,
Gas 6

Prepare ahead:
1 hour

Freeze:
No

1. Line the small shallow baking tray with Bake-O-Glide.

2. Trim and prepare the sprouts.

3. Pile into the roasting tin with the olive oil, bacon and chestnuts and shake well.

3. Hang the tin from the second set of runners and roast for 8 – 10 minutes, season and serve.

leeks in daisy's sauce

Serves 4

1 lb (450g) leeks
7 oz (200g pack) cream cheese
1 tbsp grainy mustard
Salt and pepper

Prepare ahead:
1 hour

Freeze:
No

1. Set the cream cheese onto the back of the Aga to soften. Wash the leeks and slice into ½"/1cm rounds.

2. Pile the leeks into a pan and pour over boiling water. Simmer for 5 minutes until tender.

3. Drain the leeks and keep warm. In the hot pan, melt the cheese and stir in the mustard and seasoning. Add the leeks, mix well and serve.

lemon cabbage

Serves 6 – 8

1 white cabbage
1 lemon
2 oz (55g) butter
1 tsp fresh dill
Salt and pepper

Prepare ahead:
Keep warm in simmering oven
for up to 30 minutes

Freeze:
No

1. Shred the cabbage as finely as possible, preferably in a processor, and then pile it into a large pan.
2. Pour cold water over the cabbage to cover, then bring to the boil. Drain.
3. Leaving the cabbage in a colander to drain fully, melt the butter in the still-warm pan. Grate in the lemon rind and squeeze in the juice. Snip the dill into the pan, using a pair of scissors.
4. Return the cabbage to the pan and toss together.

braised red cabbage

Serves 6 – 8

1 red cabbage
1 medium cooking apple
2 oz (55g) butter
1 medium onion
1 clove garlic
Salt and pepper
1/4 pint (140ml) apple juice

Prepare ahead:
Keep warm for an hour

Freeze:
No

1. Shred the cabbage as finely as possible, preferably in a processor. Peel, core and slice the apple.
2. Slice the onion. Melt the butter and oil together and stir in the onion and crushed garlic. Heat until sizzling on the boiling plate, then cover and transfer to the simmering oven for 15 minutes until soft.
3. Stir in the cabbage and apple and pour on the apple juice and seasoning. Bring to the boil, then once again cover and put into the simmering oven for about half an hour, or longer if you want to prepare it early

christmas pudding

The recipe makes 3 puddings – one for this year, one for next year and one to give to someone else! Each one will serve 8 – 10.

8 oz (225g) raisins
8 oz (225g) sultanas
8 oz (225g) currants
4 oz (110g) mixed candied peel
4 oz (110g) glacé cherries
4 oz (110g) dark muscovado sugar
8 oz (225g) breadcrumbs, made from brioche
6 oz (175g) self-raising flour
4 oz (110g) ground almonds
8 oz (225g) beef suet
2 tbsp mixed spice
1 nutmeg, grated
4 eggs
4 tbsp black treacle
1 pint (550ml) Guinness
2 oranges
3 lemons
3 Bramley cooking apples
1 tsp orange oil
3 tbsp brandy

Oven:
Aga simmering oven, 250F, 130C, Gas 1

Prepare ahead:
1 year!

Freeze:
No need, just store in a cool, dark cupboard in a tightly sealed bowl

1. Pile all the dry ingredients into a large bowl and mix well. Peel, core and quarter the apples, then grate into the mixture. Wash the oranges and lemons, grate the zest into the mixture. Squeeze the juice into a large jug. Add the Guinness, treacle, orange oil and eggs to the juice, mix well and pour onto the other ingredients. Stir well to combine.

2. Spoon the mixture into three, 2-pint (1 litre) pudding basins. If using plastic bowls, clip on the lids, if using china bowls, cover with pleated greaseproof paper and pleated foil, secured with string or heavy duty rubber bands.

3. Pour about 1½"/3cm of boiling water into the large roasting tin, with a couple of slices of lemon to prevent it from discolouring the tin, lift in the puddings and cover tightly with foil.

4. Cook in the simmering oven for at least 24 hours. (Alternatively, steam in a large pan, one at a time, in the simmering oven or on the hob of a conventional cooker for a minimum of 12 hours each).

5. When the puddings are cooked, remove from the tin and allow to cool.

6. Wipe the outside of the bowls clean, remove lids and trickle a tablespoon of brandy over each pudding. Replace with fresh lids and store in a safe place until Christmas.

7. To reheat, either put the bowl, wrapped in foil, into the simmering oven for 4 hours or microwave for 4 minutes before serving.

brandy butter

4 oz (110g) unsalted butter
4 oz (110g) icing sugar
Grated rind of a lemon
4 tbsp brandy

Prepare ahead:
4 days

Freeze:
Yes

1. Put the butter into a bowl and put it beside the Aga to soften for 20 minutes.

2. Whisk the butter, and add the icing sugar and lemon rind and then gradually beat in the brandy. Pile into a bowl and refrigerate until needed.

3. On Christmas Day, remove from the fridge and bring to room temperature before spooning generously over Christmas pudding or mince pies.

cumberland rum butter

4 oz (110g) unsalted butter
4 oz (110g) light muscovado sugar
Grated rind of an orange
4 tbsp dark rum

Prepare ahead:
4 days

Freeze:
Yes

1. Put the butter into a bowl and put it beside the Aga to soften for 20 minutes.

2. Whisk the butter, and add the sugar and orange rind and then gradually beat in the rum. Pile into a bowl and refrigerate until needed.

3. On Christmas Day, remove from the fridge and bring to room temperature before spooning generously over Christmas pudding or mince pies.

Try using Grand Marnier or Cointreau instead of the rum for a more orangey flavour

brandy sauce

Serves 4 – 6

1 pint (550ml) milk
1 oz (25g) caster sugar
1 oz (25g) cornflour
3 tbsp brandy

Prepare ahead:
1 hour

Freeze:
No

1. Put the sugar and cornflour into a pan and add a couple of spoons of milk. Mix together thoroughly, then pour on the rest of the milk.

2. Heat on the simmering plate, stirring all the time, until the sauce boils. Remove from the heat and stir in the brandy.

3. Cover with cling film and put into the simmering oven, or keep warm on the back of the Aga.

A variation is rum sauce: use rum instead of brandy.

Rum butter and rum sauce complement each other with the pudding, or brandy butter and brandy sauce.

This aims to have lunch on the table at 2pm. If you plan to eat later or earlier, adjust the timings accordingly.

christmas eve

1. In the morning, take from the freezer: the gravy, the bread sauce, the stuffings, bacon rolls, the mashed root vegetables and the brandy butter. Allow to thaw near the Aga, then refrigerate overnight.

2. Prepare the turkey and put it into the roasting tin and cover with foil.

3. Peel the sprouts, chop the bacon, and prepare the chestnuts (a good, time consuming job for an unskilled kitchen volunteer!) and put into a bowl together, cover and refrigerate.

4. Separate the sausages and put onto grill rack in a roasting tin, with the bacon rolls, cover and refrigerate.

5. Find the Christmas pudding in its safe place and put in a visible place!

6. Lay the table for tomorrow, remembering to put out enough serving spoons.

Late in the evening, put the turkey into the oven – see page 9 for slow cooking times.

christmas day

4.00am	Children get up and run screaming around the house.
9.30am	Parents get up and have a leisurely, cooked breakfast, lots of coffee, admiring Father Christmas's presents, etc.
10.00am	Check on the turkey, drain off some of the juices (add to the rest of the thawed gravy) and return it to the oven. Wrap the Christmas pudding in foil and tuck it into simmering oven beside the turkey. Put bread sauce in its serving dish in the simmering oven to warm through.
10.15am	Go and supervise present opening, go for a walk, go to church, etc.
11.30am	Put some sausage rolls into the roasting oven to stave off children's hunger until later.
11.45am	Serve sausage rolls to hungry children
12.40pm	Hang the tin of sausages and bacon rolls from top set of runners in the roasting oven.
12.50pm	Turn the sausages and return to the oven to brown on the other side. Make the brandy sauce, cover with cling film and leave to keep warm.
12.59pm	Glass of wine for the cook! Sausages and bacon rolls out of the oven, onto a plate in the simmering oven to keep warm.
1.00pm	Transfer the turkey, uncovered, to the roasting oven to brown. Open jar of cranberry sauce and put on table with a spoon.
1.20pm	Bring the root vegetables to the boil in their various pans, drain, cover and put into the simmering oven.
1.30pm	Take the turkey from the roasting oven and put onto a serving plate. Cover with foil and set beside the Aga to keep warm. Pour the ready-made gravy into the remaining meat juices in the roasting tin.
1.35pm	Tip frozen roast potatoes into a large roasting tin and hang from the top set of runners in the roasting oven. Tip sprouts, chestnuts and bacon into a roasting tin and hang from 3rd set of runners in the roasting oven. Put the gravy onto the floor of the roasting oven to boil.
1.45pm	Remove parsnips and celeriac from simmering oven and mash with stilton. Remove carrots from simmering oven and glaze with honey and orange. Put into serving dishes and return to simmering oven to keep warm.
1.50pm	Take sprouts and potatoes from roasting oven and put onto serving dishes. Set on the back of the Aga to keep warm. Take gravy from the oven and pour into a jug. Set on the back of the Aga to keep warm.
)pm	Carve the bird, sit down and enjoy your Christmas feast; you deserve it!

For a really relaxed Christmas Day, prepare as many of the trimmings as possible in advance:

1. Make bread sauce, slightly sloppier than normal. Freeze in plastic bags resting in tubs to make them easier to pack into the freezer. When defrosted, the sauce will be the perfect consistency, as the bread will absorb more milk as it defrosts. Reheat in the simmering oven for an hour.
2. Ask your butcher for poultry giblets and make the gravy in advance. Freeze as above. When the turkey is cooked, stir the ready made gravy into the roasting juices and boil.
3. Make brandy butter and freeze.
4. Make mincemeat and cranberry sauce: they keep in sterilised jars for a month or so and make lovely gifts, with a pretty ribbon tied around the top of the jar.
5. Prepare and ROAST the potatoes, cool and freeze. Reheat just before serving at the top of the roasting oven for 20 minutes.
6. Prepare any mashed vegetables for Christmas day and freeze. Thaw on Christmas Eve and reheat in the roasting oven for half an hour before keeping warm in the simmering oven.
7. Make stuffings and freeze in the tins they are to be cooked in. Thaw on Christmas Eve then cook in the roasting oven the next day.
8. Make cheese pastry cases, pinwheels and puffs and freeze – instant canapés ready to cook straight from the freezer.

Sometimes you just don't want a conventional Christmas dinner, there may be too few people to eat a big bird, or you simply might not fancy turkey or a rich steamed pudding this year – here are some alternative ideas.

roast goose

Serves 6 – 8

7 lb (3kg) goose
Salt and pepper
1 onion

Oven:
Aga roasting oven, 400F, 200C, Gas 6

Prepare ahead:
No

Freeze:
No

Keep the vast amount of fat that will drain off, and use it for roasting potatoes or frying bread – it will keep in the fridge for up to a month, or freeze the fat in small quantities to use throughout the coming year

1. Line the large roasting tin with Bake-O-Glide. Rub the goose with salt (to crispen the skin) and peel the onion, halve it and push it into the body cavity. Set the goose, on its breast, onto the grill rack in the large roasting tin. Hang from the lowest set of runners in the roasting oven and cook for half an hour.

2. Take from the oven, drain off the fat and turn the goose over. Return to the oven and roast for 1½ hours. It is cooked when a skewer inserted into the thigh produces clear juices. You will need to drain off the fat after about 45 minutes.

3. When your goose is cooked, remove from the oven and put onto a serving dish to keep warm. Pour off all but a couple of spoonfuls of fat and make gravy in the roasting tin, on the floor of the oven (see page 11). Serve with spiced apple sauce.

spiced apple sauce

Serves 6

1 lb (450g) cooking apples
1 oz (25g) butter
Rind and juice of a lemon
4 cloves
6 allspice berries
1 cinnamon stick
1 bay leaf

Oven:
Aga simmering oven, 250F,
130C, Gas 1

Prepare ahead:
1 week

Freeze:
Yes

1. Peel, core and slice the apples. Melt the butter in a pan on the simmering plate and add the apples, lemon rind and juice.

2. Break up the cinnamon, and bruise the cloves and berries. Tip into a muslin bag and put into the pan.

3. When the pan is sizzling, cover and put into the simmering oven for 20 minutes, until the apples are soft.

4. Remove from the oven, remove the bag of spices and beat the sauce well – straining is optional!

5. Pour into sterilised jars and seal whilst still hot, or allow to cool, then store in a plastic / Tupperware box in the fridge.

roast capon, chicken, pork, beef or lamb

Take a joint of meat – leg of lamb, topside of beef, leg of pork, capon, chicken etc. Wipe the joint with kitchen paper to dry.

Rub pork skin with salt for extra crispy crackling. Rub capon or chicken skin with salt, pepper and tarragon, cut up an onion and a lemon and push into the cavity. Rub mustard onto a beef joint. Make cuts in a lamb joint and push slivers of garlic and sprigs of rosemary into the meat.

Fast roasting
Line the roasting tin with Bake-O-Glide and put in the meat. Hang the tin from the third set of runners in the roasting oven and cook – 12 min per lb for beef, 20 min per lb for lamb and chicken, 25 min per lb for pork.

Medium roasting
Put the meat into the roasting oven for one third of the cooking time, to allow the joint to seal and brown, then move to the simmering oven, for the entire minutes per pound cooking time.
When cooked, remove the meat and allow to rest for at least 10 minutes to allow the juices to settle, whilst you make the gravy.

gravy

Making the gravy is often the most stressful part of cooking Christmas dinner, you stand there stirring the gravy on the heat, waiting for someone to come and lay the table for lunch or giving up and laying it yourself, while the gravy burns and goes lumpy. No longer ... cooking the gravy on the floor of the oven leaves you free to get completely organised before serving up the meal, with no stress at all!

1. Pour off all but 2 tbsp of the fat from the tin.
2. Stir in 2 tbsp flour, then blend in a pint (550ml) of stock – maybe adding a spoonful of wine – and for lamb a teaspoonful of redcurrant jelly, for beef a spoonful of Dijon mustard, for chicken some tarragon.
3. Stir well then put the tin onto the floor of the roasting oven for 5 minutes.
4. Stir and return to the oven for 5 more minutes and the gravy will be boiling and thickened, ready to stir and serve.

slow baked marmalade gammon

Serves 8 – 10

6 lb (3³/₄kg) gammon joint
¹/₂ tsp allspice berries
¹/₂ tsp cloves
¹/₂ tsp peppercorns
2–3 tbsp marmalade
2–3 tbsp demerara sugar to glaze

Oven:
Aga simmering oven, 250F, 130C, Gas 1

Prepare ahead:
Yes

Freeze:
Yes

1. Soak the joint in cold water overnight. Line the large roasting tin with foil.

2. Grind the spices together and mix with the marmalade. Smear this all over the joint and lay it into the tin. Wrap loosely and put into the simmering oven for 45 minutes per pound, 90 minutes per kilo.

3. When cooked, remove from the oven, open the package and peel away the skin. Score the fat then smear with a little more marmalade, and press on the sugar. Bake in the roasting oven for 20 minutes until glazed and browned.

4. Serve, either hot with Hampshire sauce (see page 34), or chilled.

hampshire sauce

Serves 8 – 10

1 jar (340g) crab apple or
quince jelly
1 lemon
1 tbsp Dijon mustard
½ medium onion
¼ pint (150ml) sweet sherry
1 tsp arrowroot

Prepare ahead:
4 days

Freeze:
No

1. Tip the contents of the jar into a pan.
2. Peel the onion and grate it on a very fine grater. Grate the rind of the lemon and squeeze the juice. Mix together the sherry, mustard and arrowroot, then stir into the pan, together with the lemon juice, rind and onion.
3. Set onto the simmering plate and gently bring to the boil, stirring all the time – the jelly will melt and dissolve and the arrowroot will thicken the sauce.
4. Pour into a jug and serve.

chocolate christmas pudding

Serves 8

6 oz (180g) mixed dried sour cherries, blueberries and raisins
Grated rind of an orange
3 tbsp brandy
3 tbsp double cream
12 oz (375g) plain chocolate
7 oz (200g tub) cream cheese
7 oz (200g pack) ratafia biscuits

To serve:
¼ pint (150ml) whipping cream
2 tbsp grated chocolate

Prepare ahead:
48 hours

Freeze:
Yes, but the biscuits will disintegrate into the chocolate after a week!

1. Line a 1½ pint / 900ml pudding basin with cling film.

2. Put the dried fruit into a bowl with the brandy, stir in the orange rind, cover and set aside to marinate, overnight if possible.

3. Set the cream cheese onto the back of the Aga to soften. Melt the chocolate and cream together in a bowl on the back of the Aga. Beat the cream cheese into the chocolate mixture. Stir in the brandy and fruit. Crush the biscuits, fold into the pudding and pour into the prepared bowl. Chill overnight.

4. To serve, turn out onto a plate. Beat the cream until sloppy then pour over the pudding. Scatter over the grated chocolate and serve.

chilled cranberry christmas pudding

Serves 6 – 8

3 tbsp honey
2 tbsp water
6 oz (175g) cranberries – fresh or frozen
12 oz (350g) cream cheese
¼ pint (150ml) soured cream
3 tbsp rosehip syrup or rose water
1 tbsp orange juice

Sauce:
2 tbsp honey
2 tbsp water
2 tbsp orange juice
6 oz (175g) cranberries
1 tbsp cornflour

Mint leaves to garnish

Prepare ahead:
Yes

Freeze:
Yes, you can serve it still half frozen like an ice cream!

1. Put the honey, water and cranberries into a pan and simmer for 10 minutes, until the cranberries are soft. Allow to cool. Set the cream cheese onto the back of the Aga to soften.

2. Whizz the fruit in a processor, and add the remaining ingredients. Whizz until well mixed.

3. Line a 2 pint / 1 litre pudding basin with cling film and pour in the mixture. Chill for at least 4 hours or freeze.

4. *For the sauce:* Put the honey, water, orange juice and cranberries into a pan on the simmering plate, bring to the boil and simmer for 5 minutes. Mix the cornflour with a spoonful of water and add to the pan and stir gently over the heat until thickened and boiled. Leave to cool.

5. Dip the basin into a bowl of hot water, then turn out onto a plate. Pour over some of the cold sauce and serve the rest of the sauce separately.

screaming panic, we've-forgotten-the-christmas-pudding, emergency pudding

Serves 6

Not cooked in the Aga but very useful in a crisis!

4 oz (110g) butter
4 oz (110g) dark brown sugar
4 oz (110g) self raising flour
½ tsp mixed spice
1 egg
2 tbsp ruby port
1 tsp gravy browning
6 oz (175g) mixed dried fruit
4 oz (110g) carrot, grated

To serve:
2 tbsp brandy, brandy butter, brandy sauce etc etc

Oven:
650W microwave

Prepare ahead:
Obviously not!

1. Put the butter, flour, sugar, egg, mixed spice, port and gravy browning into a processor and whizz until smoothly combined. Add the fruit and carrot and whizz briefly to combine.

2. Grease a 2 pint (1 litre) pudding basin and pour the mixture into it. Microwave for 6 minutes on high. Allow to stand for 5 minutes before turning out.

3. Heat the brandy in a ladle and pour over, then apply a match and carry, flaming, to the table, as if nothing were the matter!

leek and yum pie

Serves 6

1½ lb (600g) leeks
8 oz (225g) yam or sweet
potato
7 oz (200g) packet filo pastry
2 oz (50g) butter
6 oz (175g) mozzarella cheese
1 cooking apple
Juice of ½ lemon
Salt and pepper

Oven:
Aga 4th runners of roasting
oven or 2nd runners of baking
oven, 170C, 350F, Gas 4

Prepare ahead:
24 hours

Freeze:
Yes

1. Set the butter in a bowl on the back of the Aga to melt.

2. Peel the yam or sweet potato and cut into ½"/5mm slices. Put into a pan of water, bring to the boil, then drain, cover and put into the simmering oven for 15–20 minutes until soft.

3. Slice the leeks into ½"/1cm rings, wash thoroughly and boil for 10 minutes until soft. Drain and allow to cool.

4. Lay 4 sheets of filo pastry into a 10" (25cm) loose-based cake tin, with the edges hanging over.

5. Pile the leeks and yams into the tin, in layers. Season well.

6. Cut the cheese into ¼"/5mm dice and sprinkle over. Peel, core and dice the apple, toss in lemon juice and add to the pie.

7. Fold the edges of the pastry over the pie and scrumple up the remaining sheets and put them on top. Brush with melted butter and bake for 20–30 minutes; you may need to slide in the cold plain shelf over the pie after 20 minutes if it looks too browned.

8. Serve warm or cold with salad and crusty bread.

spinach and three cheese strudel

Serves 4 – 6

4 sheets filo pastry
2 tbsp olive oil
1 onion
12 oz (340g) spinach, washed
7 oz (200g pack) cream cheese
4 oz (110g) feta cheese
2 oz (55g) grated fresh
parmesan cheese
2 tbsp chopped fresh parsley
Grated nutmeg
Salt and pepper

Oven:
Aga floor of roasting oven 350F,
170C, Gas 4

Prepare ahead:
24 hours uncooked

Freeze:
Yes, uncooked

1. Stand the cream cheese on the back of the Aga to soften.

2. Peel and chop the onion. Heat 1 tbsp of olive oil in a pan and heat the onion until sizzling. Cover and put into the simmering oven for 15 minutes to soften. Add the spinach and cook quickly, shaking occasionally, until all the water has evaporated. Draw off the heat and allow to cool.

3. Crumble the feta, and add it, with the other cheeses, parsley, seasoning and a good grating of nutmeg, to the pan. Mix thoroughly.

4. Line the cold plain shelf with Bake-O Glide. Lay a sheet of pastry onto it, brush with a little of the remaining oil, then lay another sheet on top. Continue oiling and laying the sheets of pastry until it is all used up.

5. Pile the spinach mixture onto the centre of the pastry, spreading to within an inch (2cm) of the edges. Roll up into a sausage, pinching the edges together. Brush with a little more oil.

6. Cook for 20–25 minutes until golden brown (you may need to use the cold plain shelf for the last 7–10 minutes if it is browning too quickly). Serve with a mixed salad.

spring onion and watercress tart

Serves 6

6 oz (175g) plain flour
3 oz (85g) butter
1 tbsp grated parmesan cheese
2 – 3 tbsp water
½ oz (10g) butter
1 bunch spring onions
1 bunch watercress
3 eggs
5 fl oz (150ml) milk
4 oz (110g) cheddar cheese
Salt and pepper

Oven:
Aga roasting oven, 400F, 200C,
Gas 6

Prepare ahead:
24 hours

Freeze:
Yes

1. To make the pastry, put the flour, butter and parmesan into a processor and whizz until the texture of breadcrumbs. With the motor running, add the water a spoonful at a time until it comes together as a dough.

2. Roll out the pastry and line a 9"/23cm flan dish. Chill until required.

3. For the filling, trim and slice the spring onions, wash and roughly chop the watercress.

4. Grate the cheddar cheese into a bowl. Add the eggs and milk with a little salt and pepper and beat together. Stir in the onions and watercress. Pour into the prepared flan case and put onto the floor of the roasting oven for 25 minutes until set and golden.

kate's garden pasta

Serves 4

12 oz (325g) pasta bows
4 oz (110g) cherry tomatoes
Good handful rocket leaves
1 clove garlic
2 tbsp olive oil
Salt and pepper
2 tbsp grated fresh parmesan cheese

Prepare ahead: 5 minutes

Freeze: No

1. Bring a large pan of water to the boil and cook the pasta according to the instructions on the packet. When cooked, drain.

2. Whilst the pasta is cooking, peel and crush the garlic and wash and quarter the tomatoes.

3. Pour the oil into the still-warm pasta pan; add the garlic, tomatoes, rocket and cheese. Season well. Pour the drained pasta back into the pan, stir together and serve at once.

not quite ratatouille

Serves 4 – 6

3 medium courgettes
1 onion
1 clove garlic
1 tbsp olive oil
1 oz (25g) butter
½ pint (275ml) tomato passata
1 tsp caster sugar
Salt and pepper

Oven:
Aga simmering oven, 250F,
130C, Gas 1

Prepare ahead:
Will keep warm for half an hour

Freeze:
Yes

1. Wash the courgettes and cut into
   ½"/1cm cubes. Peel and chop the
   onion, crush the garlic.

2. Heat the oil and butter in a heavy pan on
   the boiling plate, add the onion and garlic
   and stir over the heat for 2 minutes. Add
   the courgettes and continue to cook for
   another 2 minutes.

3. Pour on the passata, season with salt,
   pepper and sugar. Bring to the boil then
   cover and put into the simmering oven
   for 5–10 minutes until the courgettes are
   cooked but not soggy.

pasta with spinach and red peppers

Serves 4

8 oz (225g) penne pasta
8 oz (225g) fresh spinach
2 red peppers
1 orange
Tabasco sauce (optional)
Salt and pepper
Fresh parmesan cheese

Oven:
Aga roasting oven, 400F, 200C,
Gas 6

Prepare ahead:
sauce, 24 hours

Freeze:
sauce, yes

1. Put the peppers into a roasting tin and roast for 25 minutes, until blackened. Leave to cool.

2. Remove the skin from the peppers, cut open and remove the seeds. Squeeze the juice from the oranges and whizz, with the peppers and a few drops of Tabasco to taste.

3. Bring a large pan of water to the boil and cook the pasta according to the instructions on the packet. When cooked, stir in the spinach then drain at once.

4. Pour the pepper sauce into the still-warm pan and heat gently. Add the pasta and spinach and stir together. Serve at once, shaving some parmesan over the top.

aubergine gratin

Serves 4

2 aubergines
5 oz (140g) mozzarella
Handful fresh oregano or basil
7 fl oz (200ml) tomato passata
1 oz (25g) grated fresh
parmesan
Salt and pepper

Oven temp:
Aga roasting oven, 400F, 200C,
Gas 6

Prepare ahead:
1 hour

Freeze:
before baking, yes

1. Wash the aubergines and cut into $1/4$"/$1/2$ cm rounds.

2. Heat a grill pan for 5 minutes in the roasting oven, then cook the aubergine slices in batches for 3 minutes. Turn each slice and cook for 3 minutes more, until browned on both sides.

3. Cut the mozzarella into thin slices. Chop the oregano or basil – you need about 2 tbsp.

4. Put some of the cooked aubergine slices into a wide, shallow dish, to cover the base. Lay on a few slices of mozzarella, scatter with oregano, salt and pepper then pour over some passata. Continue to add alternate layers of aubergine, cheese, oregano and passata, finishing with aubergines.

5. Scatter with the grated parmesan and cook at the top of the roasting oven for 15 minutes until golden and bubbling.

souffléd cauliflower cheese

Serves 4

1 medium cauliflower
1 oz (25g) butter
1 oz (25g) plain flour
³/₄ pint (425ml) milk
2 eggs
3 oz (75g) cheddar cheese
Salt and pepper

Oven:
Aga roasting oven, 400F, 200C,
Gas 6

Prepare ahead:
1 hour

Freeze:
before baking

1. Break the cauliflower into florets and put into a deep pan, cover with water and put onto the boiling plate. When boiling, move across to the simmering plate and simmer for 5 minutes until tender. Drain and pile into a soufflé dish (2 pint / 1 litre). Put into the simmering oven to keep warm while you make the sauce.

2. Melt the butter in the still-warm pan and stir in the flour. Slowly add the milk, stirring all the time. Set onto the simmering plate and bring to the boil, stirring. Grate the cheese and separate the eggs. Remove the sauce from the heat and stir in the cheese and egg yolks. Whisk the egg whites until stiff, then fold them into the sauce.

3. Pour over the cauliflower and then cook in the centre of the roasting oven for 15–20 minutes until puffed up and golden.

cooked breakfast, including aga toast

For each person, at least

1 sausage
2 rashers bacon
1 tomato
1 field mushroom
1 egg
1 slice bread

Oven:
Aga roasting oven, 400F, 200C, Gas 6

Prepare ahead:
Put everything into the roasting tin the night before, ready to put straight into the oven in the morning!

Freeze:
No

1. Line the large roasting tin with Bake-O-Glide. Halve the tomatoes and lay them in the tin. Place the sausages on the grill rack and put it in the tin. Hang the tin from the highest set of runners and cook for 10 minutes. Turn the sausages then add the bacon to the rack and the mushrooms in the base of the tin. Cook for a further 12–15 minutes.

2. Meanwhile, heat the toaster then make some toast. Cut a hole in the centre of each slice of toast.

3. When the sausages, bacon, tomatoes and mushrooms are cooked, remove from the tin and arrange on a plate. Keep warm in the simmering oven.

4. Put the toast into the tin and break the egg into it. Cook on the base of the oven for 2–3 minutes until the yolk is set. Serve at once.

fat free 'fried' eggs

Lay a sheet of Bake-O-Glide on the simmering plate, then break an egg onto it. It will 'fry' in a couple of minutes, using no fat at all. Lower the lid to reflect the heat back and cook the top of the egg – it will set and you avoid the slimy white you so often get with a 'runny' yolk. You can fry up to three eggs at a time on the simmering plate – brilliant!

the aga kettle

Make sure that the boiling plate is free of crumbs and the base of the kettle clean, so that there is really good contact between the two – this way the kettle boils very quickly. The kettle boils so fast that it makes sense to draw fresh cold water every time you use the kettle, thus avoiding it scaling up too fast.

aga toast

The secret to making successful toast on the Aga is to heat the toaster before you start. Slide it under the boiling plate lid for a couple of minutes before putting in the slices of bread. Toast cooks very quickly, so beware answering the door or the telephone when your bread is toasting!

The Aga 'bat' toaster has two 'settings', the right way out for thick toast, crumpets, muffins, teacakes, toasted sandwiches, etc, when it makes sense to cook the toast more gently on the simmering plate, where the heat is gentler and less likely to burn. The 'inside out' setting is for thinner slices of bread, which toast very efficiently on the boiling plate, under a lowered lid.

Once you have finished making toast, make sure that the plate is free of crumbs, otherwise the next time you try to cook anything it will not make complete contact with the plate for good heat transfer.

porridge

Serves 4

8 oz (225g) porridge oats
5 fl oz (150ml) milk
10 fl oz (300ml) water

To serve:
Double cream
Soft brown sugar or
maple syrup

Prepare ahead:
12 hours on back of Aga

1. Put the oats, water and milk into a pan, cover and set on the back of the Aga overnight.

2. *I find that if the pan spends the night in the simmering oven, the porridge tends to thicken and set like concrete.*

3. In the morning, move the pan onto the simmering plate, where it will boil extremely quickly. Simmer for a couple of minutes and serve.

4. If making porridge from scratch in the morning, it will need to simmer for at least 5 minutes for the oats to soften.

pancakes with maple syrup

Makes about 4 medium pancakes or 6 small ones

4 oz (110g) self raising flour
1 tsp baking powder
1 tbsp caster sugar
1 egg
3 – 4 fl oz (100 – 140ml) milk

To serve:
2 tbsp crème fraîche
maple syrup

Prepare ahead:
No

Freeze:
No

1. Beat together the flour, baking powder, sugar, egg and milk.

2. *If you like thick pancakes, use less milk for a thicker mixture; if you prefer them thinner, use more milk.*

3. Lay a sheet of Bake-O-Glide on the simmering plate and spoon the mixture onto it, leaving plenty of room around each pancake.

4. Once they bubble and set, turn with a palate knife and cook on the other side – they take a total of about 4 minutes.

5. Pile on a plate and serve with a blob of crème fraîche on each and maple syrup poured over.

bacon pinwheels

Makes about 25 pinwheels

8 oz (225g) pack puff pastry
about 12 rashers streaky bacon
3 tbsp Dijon mustard

Oven:
Aga centre of roasting oven,
400F, 200C, Gas 6

Prepare ahead:
24 hours

Freeze:
Yes, uncooked

1. Roll the pastry out to a rectangle, about ¼"/5mm thick and spread with mustard. Lay the slices of bacon across the pastry and roll up tightly. Cut into ¼"/5mm slices and place on a baking sheet, covered with Bake-O-Glide.

2. Bake for about 10–12 minutes until puffed and golden. Serve hot.

smoked salmon pinwheels

Makes about 25 pinwheels

Exactly the same method as for bacon pinwheels, but use 8 oz (225g) smoked salmon slices and a spoonful of dill sauce instead of the bacon and mustard.

cheese crispies

Makes about 20

4 oz (110g) mature Cheddar
2 oz (55g) ready salted crisps
2 oz (55g) plain flour
2 oz (55g) butter

Oven temp:
Aga 4th runners of roasting oven
or 2nd runners of baking oven,
375F, 190C, Gas 5

Prepare ahead: 12 hours

Freeze: uncooked

1. Set the butter into a large bowl on the back of the Aga to melt.

2. Grate the cheese and crush the crisps. Mix together in to the butter and add the flour. Mix to form a dough.

3. Place heaped teaspoonfuls onto a greased baking sheet. Flatten gently with the back of a spoon and bake for 10 minutes.

4. Cool on a rack and serve.

smoked cod and caviar roulade

Makes about 40 slices

5 oz (150g) smoked cod fillet
4 eggs
Salt & pepper

Filling:
Salt & pepper
1 tbsp lumpfish caviar
7 oz (200g) cream cheese
Grated rind of a lemon

Oven temp:
Aga 4th runners of roasting oven or 2nd runners of baking oven, 350F, 180C, Gas 4

Prepare ahead:
24 hours

Freeze:
Yes, wrapped in kitchen paper to absorb moisture

1. Line the large roasting tin with Bake-O-Glide. Set the pack of cream cheese on the back of the Aga to soften.

2. Separate eggs and whizz smoked cod, seasoning and yolks together to a paste. Whisk whites and fold into fish mixture. Spread over the tin and bake for 15 minutes.

3. When the roulade is cooked, turn out onto a tea towel, remove paper and cut in half lengthways. Roll each half up in the towel, to create long sausages. Allow to cool.

4. Beat the cream cheese with the caviar and lemon rind. Unroll the roulades and spread with the filling. Roll up tightly in the tea towel and chill for at least 4 hours.

5. To serve, cut into $1/2$"/1cm slices and arrange on a plate.

tomato and pesto roulade

Makes about 40 slices

3 tbsp sun dried tomato purée
4 eggs
Salt & pepper

Filling:
Salt & pepper
2 tbsp pesto sauce
8 oz (225g) cream cheese

Oven:
Aga 4th runners of roasting
oven or 2nd runners of baking
oven, 350F, 180C, Gas 4

Prepare ahead:
24 hours

Freeze:
No

1. Line the large roasting tin with Bake-O-Glide. Separate eggs and mix tomato purée, seasoning and yolks together. Whisk whites and fold into mixture. Spread over the tin and bake for 8 minutes. When the roulade is cooked, turn out onto a tea towel, remove paper and cut in half lengthways. Roll each half up in the towel, to create long sausages. Allow to cool.

2. Beat the cream cheese with the pesto and then unroll the roulades and spread with the filling. Roll up tightly in the tea towel and chill for at least 4 hours. To serve, cut into $1/2$"/1cm slices and arrange on a plate.

smoked mackerel puffs

Makes 24

1 lb (450g) puff pastry
1 egg

Filling:
4 oz (110g) smoked mackerel
4 oz (110g) cream cheese
2 tsp horseradish sauce
Salt and pepper
Grated rind and juice 1 lemon

Oven:
Aga centre of roasting oven,
400F, 200C, Gas 6

Prepare ahead:
24 hours, uncooked

Freeze:
Yes, uncooked

1. Mix together (in a processor) the fish, cheese, horseradish, lemon and seasoning.

2. Roll out the pastry to $\frac{1}{8}$"/3mm thick and lay onto a 24-hole mini muffin tin. Brush with beaten egg.

3. Put about $\frac{2}{3}$ teaspoon of the fish mixture into each dip, then fold over the remaining pastry and press down the edges to seal with the rolling pin. Flip the tin over to release the pastry, then cut out the puffs with a 2"/5cm cutter.

4. Brush with beaten egg, lay onto a baking sheet and bake for 12–15 minutes, until risen and browned. Serve warm.

cheese, walnut and olive traybake

Makes 32 small squares

8 oz (225g) self raising flour
1 tsp baking powder
3 oz (85g) butter
3 eggs
2 oz (55g) walnut pieces
3 oz (85g) grated cheddar cheese
2 oz (55g) stoned black olives

Oven:
Aga 4th runners of roasting oven or 3rd runners of baking oven, 375F, 190C, Gas 5

Prepare ahead:
24 hours

Freeze:
Yes

1. Line the small roasting tin with Bake-O-Glide. Put the grid shelf on to the floor of the roasting oven.

2. Pile the flour, butter, baking powder, eggs and cheese into a processor and whizz to mix. Add the olives and walnuts then, using the pulse button, briefly mix together.

3. Tip into the tin, smooth the top then bake.

4. <u>2 oven Aga:</u> Set the small roasting tin full of mixture into the large roasting tin and hang from the 4th runners in the roasting oven, with the cold plain shelf on the 2nd runners. Bake for 25 minutes until risen and browned.

5. <u>3 and 4 oven Aga:</u> Hang the tin from the 3rd runners in the baking oven and cook for 25 – 30 minutes until risen and browned.

6. Cool on a rack then cut into 1"/3cm squares and serve.

salmorejo dip

1 large clove garlic
1 red pepper
4 medium tomatoes
4 oz (110g) white bread, crusts removed
10 tbsp Spanish olive oil
Salt and pepper

Prepare ahead:
up to 36 hours

Freeze:
No

1. Put the tomatoes into a bowl; pour over boiling water and leave to stand for a minute. Remove the skins. Quarter the tomatoes and discard the core and seeds.

2. Peel the garlic. Wash the pepper and cut into chunks, discarding the core and seeds.

3. Pile the vegetables into a processor. Add the bread and whizz. With the motor running, pour the olive oil into the mixture. Season.

4. Pour into a bowl, cover and refrigerate for at least 12 hours for the flavours to develop.

5. Serve with chunks of bread or vegetables to dip in.

avocado and watercress dip

1 bunch watercress
2 avocados
Handful fresh parsley
2 spring onions
1 clove garlic
1 lemon
Handful fresh basil leaves
4 tbsp olive oil
Salt and pepper

Prepare ahead:
12 hours

Freeze:
No

1. Wash and dry the watercress. Pile it into a processor.

2. Trim the spring onions and cut into chunks. Halve, peel and de-stone the avocados. Grate the rind of the lemon and squeeze the juice. Add these to the processor, with the basil, salt and pepper.

3. Whizz and then, with the motor still running, slowly pour in the olive oil until it emulsifies.

creamy tomato dip

7 oz (200g pack) cream cheese
2 tbsp sun dried tomato purée
1 tbsp chopped fresh basil
Salt and pepper

Prepare ahead:
12 hours

Freeze:
No

1. Stand the cream cheese on the back of the Aga to soften for half an hour.

2. Mix together the cream cheese and tomato purée, season to taste and stir in the basil.

3. Pour into a bowl, cover and refrigerate for at least 2 hours for the flavours to develop.

4. Serve with chunks of bread or vegetables to dip.

cheese pastry cases

Makes about 48

8 oz (225g) plain flour
2 oz (55g) grated cheddar
4 oz (110g) butter
Pinch of mustard powder
Salt and pepper
2–3 tbsp cold water

Oven temp:
Aga 4th runners of roasting
oven, 400F, 200C, Gas 6

Prepare ahead:
48 hours

Freeze:
Yes, brilliantly! Just take them
out of the freezer and fill. By the
time they are on the plate, they
have defrosted

1. Whizz all ingredients together to form a
   dough. Wrap in cling film and chill for $1/2$
   hour. Roll out as thinly as possible, and
   using a 2"/5cm cutter, cut into rounds.

2. Line mini muffin tins with the pastry. Prick
   with a fork and chill for 20 minutes.

3. Bake in the centre of the roasting oven
   for about 5 minutes until golden. Turn
   onto a cooling rack.

Once cold, fill with ...

turkey liver pâté

8 oz (225g) turkey liver
8 oz (225g) butter
2 cloves garlic
Handful fresh tarragon
2 tbsp brandy
7 oz (200g pack) cream cheese

Prepare ahead:
24 hours, out of cases

Freeze:
Yes, out of the pastry cases!

1. Set the cream cheese onto the back of the Aga to soften.

2. Peel and crush the garlic. Melt the butter in a large pan and add the livers and garlic. Cook on the floor of the roasting oven for about 10 minutes, then cover and transfer to the simmering oven for a further 10 minutes. Allow to cool.

3. Pour into food processor and whizz until smooth. Add a handful of tarragon and the cream cheese, then whizz again, until it is well incorporated. Chill for about an hour, until thickened but not set.

4. Fill a plastic bag with pâté, snip one corner and pipe a swirl into each case. Chill for about an hour to set. Garnish with a tarragon leaf.

or ...

1. Chop hard boiled eggs, mix with a spoonful of mayonnaise and pile into the pastry cases. Garnish with a few lumpfish caviar eggs.

2. Mix a teaspoonful of pesto with a couple of tablespoons of mayonnaise. Spoon a small amount into the pastry cases and top with halved cherry tomatoes.

3. Fill a plastic bag with taramasalata, snip off a corner and pipe into the cases. Top with a sliver of black olive.

pear, parmesan and proscuitto salad

Serves 4

4 small William pears
12 slices proscuitto
2½ oz (60g pack) parmesan cheese
1 lime
4 tbsp olive oil
Salt and pepper
Pack (100g) mixed salad leaves

Prepare ahead:
30 minutes

Freeze:
No

1. Grate the rind of the lime and squeeze the juice into a large salad bowl. Season and stir in the olive oil.

2. Wash the pears, dry them then cut into quarters. Remove the core and slice, lengthways. Toss in the lime juice dressing.

3. Add the salad and toss together.

4. Pile onto four plates, then lay strips of proscuitto on each.

5. Using a coarse grater, grate the cheese onto each plate of salad and serve at once.

smoked trout salad

Serves 4

4 fillets hot-smoked trout
2 William pears
1 head of radicchio lettuce
2 oz (55g) rocket leaves
Salt and pepper
2 tbsp French dressing
3 tbsp crème fraîche
2 tsp creamed horseradish

Prepare ahead:
1 hour – do not dress the salad leaves until ready to eat

Freeze:
No

1. Remove the skin from the fish and break up into chunks.

2. Wash and dry the pears, quarter and remove the core. Cut into slices lengthways. Wash and dry the salad leaves. Tear the radicchio leaves into strips.

3. Pile everything into a salad bowl, pour over the French dressing and toss together.

4. For the sauce, mix the crème fraîche with the horseradish and pour over each plateful of salad. Serve with crusty bread.

somerset rarebit

Serves 4

2 English Cox's apples
4 slices wholemeal bread
5 oz (150g) cheddar
1 oz (25g) butter
Salt and pepper

Oven:
Aga roasting oven, 400F, 200C,
Gas 6

Prepare ahead:
15 minutes

Freeze:
No

1. Quarter the apples, remove the core and cut into thin slices. Grate the cheese.

2. Heat the Aga toaster on the boiling plate for 2 minutes. Put in the bread and toast on one side only. Take out the toast and spread butter on the un-toasted side. Lay the apple slices on the toast. Grate a little pepper over the top, sprinkle with salt then cover with the grated cheese.

3. Put the rarebits onto the grill rack over the roasting tin and hang from the top set of runners in the roasting oven for 5 minutes, until the cheese is melted and golden.

chilled avocado and coconut soup

Serves 4 – 6,
Wonderfully refreshing after overeating at Christmas!

½ pint (275ml) stock
4 spring onions
1 clove garlic
1 green chilli
A good handful fresh coriander
2 avocados
½ pint (275ml) Greek yogurt
¼ pint (150ml) coconut milk
1 tbsp olive oil
½ tsp caster sugar
½ lemon
Salt and pepper
More coriander leaves to garnish

Prepare ahead:
3 hours

Freeze:
No

1. Trim the onions, garlic, coriander and chilli and pile into a processor.

2. Halve, peel and de-stone the avocados and add to the processor, with the yogurt, sugar, oil, salt and pepper.

3. Whizz everything together, then add the stock and coconut milk and whizz until blended.

4. Chill for at least an hour before serving.

shirley's mushrooms

Life is NOT too short for these stuffed mushrooms!

Serves 4

4 large field mushrooms
1 tbsp olive oil
1 small onion
2 cloves garlic
3 rashers smoked back bacon
1 slice bread
1 tbsp fresh parsley
2 tbsp pine kernels
4 oz (110g) Stilton cheese

Oven:
Aga roasting oven, 400F, 200C,
Gas 6

Prepare ahead:
Keep warm for up to an hour

Freeze:
No, the mushrooms go soggy!

1. Line a small roasting tin with Bake-O-Glide.

2. Wipe the mushrooms, remove the stalks and put them into the tin.

3. Peel and chop the onion and mushroom stalks, cut the bacon into small chunks, peel and crush the garlic (in a processor, all together, is fastest!). Put the oil, onion, mushroom stalks, bacon and garlic into a pan and cook on the floor of the roasting oven for 5–8 minutes until beginning to brown.

4. Whizz the bread with the parsley; add the cooked onion and bacon mixture and pine kernels and pulse until mixed. Put spoonfuls of this onto the mushrooms, pressing down into the bowl of the mushrooms.

5. Cut the cheese into slices and lay on top of the stuffing in the mushrooms. Hang the tin from the top set of runners in the roasting oven for 10 minutes until the cheese is melted and bubbling.

red pepper cups

Serves 6

4 oz (110g) butter
2 red peppers
2 onions
2 cloves garlic
1 lb (450g) tomatoes
1 tsp caster sugar
Salt and pepper
Handful of torn basil leaves
1/4 pint (150ml) double cream
1 tin anchovies (optional)
3 tbsp grated fresh parmesan cheese

Oven:
Aga simmering oven, 250F, 130C, Gas 1 and roasting oven 400F, 200C, Gas 6

Prepare ahead:
24 hours – but brown the cheese at the last minute

Freeze:
Yes

1. Butter 6 ramekin dishes.
2. Halve the peppers and remove the seeds. Chop roughly. Peel and chop the onions and garlic.
3. Melt the butter in a pan on the simmering plate and tip in the pepper, onions and garlic and stir together until sizzling. Cover and put into the simmering oven for 20 minutes.
4. Boil a kettle of water and pour over the tomatoes. Leave for a minute then remove the skins. Chop roughly and add to the pepper pan – put it onto the boiling plate until it is boiling again then place, uncovered, on the floor of the roasting oven for 15 minutes to reduce, stirring occasionally.
5. Season with sugar, salt and pepper and add the basil. Spoon into the ramekin dishes.
6. Open the tin of anchovies and drain, then cut into 1/2"/1cm pieces. Divide between the ramekins. Pour over the cream then sprinkle on the cheese.
7. Put the ramekins into a roasting tin and hang from the top set of runners in the roasting oven for 10 minutes until browned and bubbling.

fresh tomato soup

Serves 4 – 6

1 lb (450g) tomatoes
1 onion
1 clove garlic
1 medium potato
1 pint (550ml) turkey stock
Salt and pepper
1 tsp caster sugar

Basil leaves and single cream
to garnish

Oven:
Aga simmering oven, 250F,
130C, Gas 1

Prepare ahead:
Yes

Freeze:
Yes

1. Peel and chop the onion and potato,
    crush the garlic. Melt the butter in a pan
    on the simmering plate. Add the onions,
    potato and garlic and stir together until
    sizzling. Cover and put into the
    simmering oven for 15 minutes until soft.

2. Roughly chop the tomatoes and add to
    the pan. Season with salt, pepper and
    sugar and bring to the boil. Cover and
    return to the simmering oven for 15
    minutes.

3. Strain the soup through a Mouli-lègumes
    or whizz in a blender.

4. Serve with a swirl of cream in the bowl
    and a few torn basil leaves on the top.

creamy onion soup

Serves 4 – 6

3 medium onions
2 medium potatoes
1 oz (25g) butter
1 pint (550ml) stock
½ pint (275ml) creamy milk
Salt and pepper
To serve:
¼ pint (150ml) cream
2 tbsp chopped parsley

Oven:
Aga simmering oven, 250F,
130C, Gas 1

Prepare ahead:
24 hours

Freeze:
Yes

1. Peel and chop the onion and potatoes.
2. Melt the butter in a pan on the simmering plate and cook the onions and potatoes until sizzling, then cover and put into the simmering oven for 10 minutes to soften.
3. Pour on the stock, season and bring to the boil then re-cover and return to the simmering oven for 30 minutes.
4. Whizz or sieve the soup and return to the pan. Stir in the milk and bring back to the boil. Season and serve, with a swirl of cream and a scattering of chopped parsley.

smoked mackerel, potato and cucumber salad

Serves 4

3 fillets smoked mackerel
1 large white potato
1 cucumber
2 spring onions
3 tbsp mayonnaise
1 clove garlic
1 tbsp chopped fresh parsley
Salt and pepper
Mixed leaves to serve

Oven:
Aga simmering oven, 250F,
130C, Gas 1

Prepare ahead:
6 hours, but do not add
mayonnaise until ready to serve

Freeze:
No

1. Peel the potato and cut into 1"/2 cm dice. Bring to the boil, drain, cover and put into the simmering oven for 20 minutes until soft. Allow to cool. Put into a large salad bowl.

2. Remove the skin from the fish and put into the bowl, breaking it up a little.

3. Cut the cucumber into sticks, about 2"/5cm x ¼"/½ cm and slice the spring onions thinly. Add to the bowl.

4. Crush the garlic into the mayonnaise, add the parsley, season and mix well then stir into the salad. Serve piled onto lettuce leaves, with crusty bread.

smoked cod soufflé

Serves 6 as a starter, or 4 as a main course

12 oz (330g) smoked cod
½ pint (275ml) milk
2 oz (50g) butter
1 oz (25g) plain flour
Grated rind of a lemon
2 tbsp grated parmesan
Salt and cayenne pepper
4 eggs

Oven:
Aga roasting oven, 400F, 200C,
Gas 6

Prepare ahead:
uncooked, 2 hours

Freeze:
Yes, uncooked, especially in
individual ramekin dishes

1. Grease a 2 pint (1 litre) soufflé dish. Put the fish into the dish and pour on the milk. Hang the grid shelf from the lowest set of runners in the roasting oven, put the dish on the shelf and cook the fish for 15 minutes. Remove from the dish; remove skin and flake into a bowl.

2. Melt the butter and stir in the flour. Blend in the milk and bring to the boil, stirring all the time. Remove from the heat and stir in the fish, lemon rind, seasoning and cheese. Separate the eggs and beat in the yolks. Whisk the whites and fold in to the mixture. Pour into the prepared dish and bake for 30 minutes until well risen and golden.

mum's orange chicken

Serves 4

4 chicken breasts
1 orange
2 tbsp tomato tapenade
1 clove garlic

Oven temp:
Aga roasting oven, 400F, 200C,
Gas 6

Prepare ahead:
24 hours, before cooking

Freeze:
Yes

1. Grate the rind from the orange and squeeze the juice. Crush the garlic.

2. Pile the orange rind and juice, garlic, chicken and tomato tapenade into a roasting bag. Seal tightly and rub between your hands to coat all the chicken in the sauce. Marinate for at least an hour, or overnight.

3. Put the chicken, in its bag, into a roasting tin and hang from the third set of runners in the roasting oven for 25 minutes, then tip out of the bag into a serving dish.

4. Serve with rice and a green vegetable.

honey-baked chicken

Serves 4 – 5

8 chicken pieces – thighs or drumsticks
2 oz (55g) butter
3 tbsp Dijon mustard
3 tbsp thick honey
3 tbsp medium sherry
Salt and pepper

Oven:
Aga roasting oven, 400F, 200C, Gas 6

Prepare ahead:
1 hour

Freeze:
No

1. Melt the butter and add the honey, mustard and sherry. Bring to the boil and simmer for 5 minutes until thickened. Season with salt and pepper.

2. Line the roasting tin with Bake-O-Glide and put the chicken pieces into it. Pour over about 2/3 of the sauce and hang from the third set of runners in the roasting oven for about 15 minutes.

3. Take the chicken out of the oven, turn the pieces over and pour on the remaining sauce. Hang from the top set of runners for 15 minutes until cooked through, browned and crispy. Serve at once.

thai lime chicken

Serves 4

1 lb (450g) chicken breasts
2" (5cm) root ginger
1 green chilli
2 cloves garlic
2 limes
8 oz (225g) tinned water chestnuts
1 tbsp sunflower oil
1/2 tsp caster sugar
3 spring onions
3 oz (90ml) coconut milk
1 tbsp Thai fish sauce
5 oz (150g) fine rice noodles

Prepare ahead:
1 hour, do not add onions or noodles until ready to serve

Freeze:
No

1. Cook the noodles according to the instructions on the packet, drain and keep warm.

2. Remove the skin from the chicken breasts and cut into 1/2" /1cm strips.

3. Peel the ginger and grate it. Peel and chop the garlic. Halve the chilli, remove seeds and stem and chop finely. Grate the zest from the limes and squeeze the juice. Drain the tin of water chestnuts and halve them.

4. Heat the oil in a heavy based pan on the boiling plate and add the chicken. Stir over the heat for a couple of minutes then add the grated ginger, grated lime rind, chopped chilli and garlic. Stir-fry for 2 minutes.

5. Add the lime juice, sugar and water chestnuts and continue to stir-fry for 2-4 minutes.

6. Trim the onions and cut into thin slices. Add to the pan, with the coconut milk, fish sauce and drained noodles. Stir over the heat until mixed and serve at once.

daisy's chicken and mangetout stir-fry

Serves 4

8 oz (225g) egg noodles, cooked and keeping warm in the simmering oven

4 boneless, skinless chicken breasts
1 tbsp sesame oil
1 tbsp sunflower oil
6 spring onions
2 cloves garlic
8 oz (225g) mangetout peas

Dressing:
2 limes
1 tbsp runny honey
1"/2cm fresh ginger
2 tbsp soy sauce
1 tbsp sesame oil

To finish:
1 tbsp sesame seeds
1 tbsp chopped coriander

Prepare ahead:
Prepare all ingredients and dressing up to 2 hours in advance, cook when needed

Freeze:
No

1. Cut the chicken breasts into thin strips. Trim and slice the spring onions. Crush the garlic. Trim then halve – lengthways – the mangetout.

2. Put a heavy, wide based pan into the roasting oven to heat for 10 minutes.

3. Make the dressing: grate the rind of the limes and squeeze the juice. Grate the ginger. Add the honey, oils and soy sauce and mix thoroughly.

4. Take the pan from the oven and put onto the boiling plate. Add the oil and when it is really hot, the chicken. Stir fry for about 3–5 minutes, then add the onions and peas and stir-fry for a further 3 minutes. Add the dressing and stir together.

5. Tip the noodles onto a plate, pour over the chicken and sprinkle with the sesame seeds and coriander. Serve at once.

glazed venison steaks

Serves 4

4 venison steaks, about 6 oz (175g) each
3 tbsp cranberry sauce
2 tbsp ruby port
1 tbsp olive oil
1 tsp allspice berries
1 tsp juniper berries
Salt and pepper

Oven:
Aga roasting oven, 400F, 200C, Gas 6

Prepare ahead:
Uncooked, 12 hours

Freeze:
Uncooked

1. Crush the juniper and allspice berries in a pestle and mortar. Pour into a bowl and mix in the cranberry sauce, port and oil.

2. Smear the resulting red mixture all over the steaks. Leave to marinate for an hour, if possible.

3. Put the steaks onto a grill rack in the roasting tin and hang from the top set of runners in the roasting oven. Cook for 10 minutes then turn, spoon over any sauce that has collected in the bottom of the tin and cook for a further 5 minutes.

4. Serve with stilton mash (see page 18) and glazed carrots (see page 20).

pheasant with marmalade

Serves 4

4 pheasant breasts
2 oz (50g) butter
2 bay leaves
1 lemon
5 fl oz (150ml) white wine
3 tbsp marmalade

Oven:
Aga roasting oven, 400F, 200C,
Gas 6

Prepare ahead:
Uncooked, 12 hours

Freeze:
Uncooked

1   Melt the butter in a heavy pan on the simmering plate. Add the pheasant breasts. Transfer to the floor of the roasting oven and roast for 8 minutes, then turn and continue cooking for a further 5 minutes. Remove from the pan and keep warm.

2. Grate the rind from the lemon and squeeze the juice. Put them, with the marmalade, wine and bay leaves into the pan and bring to the boil on the boiling plate and reduce for 5 minutes until you have a syrupy sauce, stirring all the time. Remove the bay leaves and pour the sauce over the pheasant breasts. Serve with celeriac and chestnut mash (see page 21).

spicy pheasant breasts

Serves 4

4 pheasant breasts
2 tsp harissa paste
1 tbsp olive oil
6 tbsp red wine
Salt and pepper

Oven:
Use the grill pan on the floor of
the Aga roasting oven

Prepare ahead:
24 hours

Freeze:
Yes

1. Smear the harissa paste over the pheasant breasts and leave to marinate for an hour.

2. Heat a grill pan in the roasting oven for 5 minutes. Cook the pheasant breasts on the floor of the roasting oven for 10 minutes, turn and continue cooking for a further 5 minutes, then remove from the pan and keep warm.

3. Pour the red wine into the pan and stir round to loosen all the pheasant juices, season then boil hard to reduce to a syrupy sauce. Serve with baked potatoes and a green salad.

creamy cod steaks

Serves 4

4 cod loin steaks
1 large packet Boursin cheese
1 tbsp olive oil
2 tbsp milk or sherry
Salt and pepper

Oven:
Aga roasting oven, 400F, 200C,
Gas 6

Prepare ahead:
Keep warm for up to half an
hour

Freeze:
Yes

1. Set the pack of cheese onto the back of the Aga to soften.

2. Heat the oil in a frying pan and add the cod steaks. Put the frying pan onto the floor of the roasting oven and cook for about 5 minutes, turning once.

3. Remove the fish from the pan when cooked. Open the pack of cheese and add to the still-warm pan, stirring until melted. Season and add milk or sherry to thin the sauce a little.

4. Serve the fish on a bed of rice or mashed potatoes, with the sauce poured over.

smoked haddock with horseradish butter

Serves 4

1¼ lb (600g) fillet of smoked haddock
1 tbsp sunflower oil
Small bunch fresh chives
1½ tbsp horseradish sauce
3 oz (85g) butter
Salt and pepper

Oven:
Aga roasting oven, 400F, 200C, Gas 6

Prepare ahead:
Keep the butter for up to 48 hours

Freeze:
Uncooked fish and butter

1. Put the butter into a bowl and place it beside the Aga to soften for half an hour.

2. Snip the chives into the bowl of butter, stir in the horseradish and mix well. Pile the butter onto a piece of cling film and roll into a sausage shape. Put into the freezer for 10 minutes to set.

3. Put the grill pan into the roasting oven to heat for 5 minutes.

4. Cut the haddock into four steaks and brush with oil on the skin side. Season with salt and pepper.

5. Lay the fish steaks, oiled skin side down, on the grill pan. Put the pan onto the floor of the roasting oven for 5–7 minutes.

6. Remove from the oven to a serving dish.

7. Serve with slices of chilled butter melting over the top of each steak.

scallops with herbs and garlic

Serves 4

1 lb (450g) scallops
12 oz (340g) linguine pasta

Sauce:
Good handful parsley
Good handful mint
Good handful chives
2 cloves garlic
1 lemon
2 tbsp cider vinegar
5 tbsp olive oil
1 tbsp capers
6 stoned black olives
Salt and pepper

Prepare ahead:
5 minutes

Freeze:
No

1. Remove the corals from the scallops and cut each one in half widthways.

2. Cook the pasta according to the instructions on the packet. Drain and keep warm in the simmering oven.

3. For the sauce, grate the rind of the lemon and squeeze the juice into a processor. Add the remaining ingredients and whizz until chopped and mixed, but not a purée.

4. Put a piece of Bake-O-Glide on the simmering plate and cook the scallops for 3 minutes on each side, until lightly browned and just cooked through. Remove from the heat, tip into a bowl and pour on the dressing, stirring to coat all the scallops.

5. Pile the pasta onto serving plates and serve topped with the scallops.

joanna's fat free salmon

Serves 4

4 salmon steaks
4 oz (110g) mushrooms, sliced
1 tbsp chopped parsley
1 lemon

Oven:
Aga roasting oven, 400F, 200C,
Gas 6

Prepare ahead:
Uncooked, 2 hours

Freeze:
Yes, uncooked

1. Take 4 pieces of foil, about 12"/30cm square and lay out on a work surface.

2. Put a salmon steak onto each piece of foil. Grate the zest of the lemon and squeeze the juice. Divide the mushrooms and parsley, over the salmon steaks. Seal each foil parcel, put into the roasting tin, and hang from the lowest set of runners and bake for 15 minutes until the fish is cooked.

3. Open each parcel and tip the contents of each onto a plate, on a bed of rice.

cod baked with tomato crust

Serves 4

4 cod loin steaks
4 oz (110g) sun-blush tomatoes
3 slices day-old wholemeal bread
3 oz (75g) butter
1 clove garlic
1 small onion
Salt and pepper

Oven:
Aga roasting oven, 400F, 200C, Gas 6 and Aga simmering oven, 250F, 130C, Gas 1

Prepare ahead:
24 hours

Freeze:
Yes, uncooked

1. Peel and chop the onion and garlic. Melt the butter in a heavy-based pan on the simmering plate and add the onion and garlic. Cook until sizzling, then cover and put into the simmering oven for 10 minutes.

2. When cooked, put into a processor, with the bread and tomatoes. Season. Whizz until chopped and mixed, but not a pulp.

3. Line the small roasting tin with Bake-O-Glide. Lay the pieces of fish in the tin. Gather handfuls of the tomato mixture onto each one, squeezing it together into a ball and press onto the top of each piece of fish.

4. Hang the tin from the third set of runners in the roasting oven and bake for 15 minutes.

prawn and cream cheese tart

Serves 6

6 oz (175g) plain flour
3 oz (85g) butter
1 tbsp parmesan cheese
2 – 3 tbsp water

4 oz (110g) prawns
3 oz (75g) cream cheese
3 eggs
5 fl oz (150ml) double cream
2 oz (50g) cheddar cheese
Salt and pepper

Oven:
Aga roasting oven, 400F, 200C,
Gas 6

Prepare ahead:
24 hours

Freeze:
Yes

1. Put the pack of cream cheese onto the back of the Aga to soften.

2. To make the pastry, put the flour, butter and parmesan into a processor and whizz until the texture of breadcrumbs. With the motor running, add the water a teaspoon at a time until it comes together as a dough.

3. Roll out the pastry and line an 8"/20cm flan dish. Chill until required.

4. For the filling, grate the cheddar cheese into a bowl. Add the cream cheese, cream and eggs with a little salt and pepper and beat together.

5. Tip the prawns into the prepared flan case, pour over the cream cheese and egg mixture, then put onto the floor of the roasting oven for 25 minutes until set and golden.

chicken thighs with anchovies and white wine

Serves 5 – 6

10 – 12 chicken thigh joints
1 onion
2 cloves garlic
2 tbsp olive oil
1 small tin anchovies in oil
½ pint (275ml) white wine
2 tbsp plain flour
Cayenne pepper
2 tbsp full-fat crème fraîche

Chopped parsley and marjoram

Oven:
Aga simmering oven, 250F,
130C, Gas 1

Prepare ahead:
24 hours

Freeze:
Yes

1. Remove the skin from the chicken joints. Peel and chop the onion and crush the garlic.

2. Heat the oil in a casserole pan on the simmering plate and add the chicken, onion and garlic. Transfer the pan to the floor of the roasting oven for 10 minutes to brown.

3. Move pan to simmering plate, stir in the flour then the anchovies and wine, stirring all the time. Season with cayenne pepper (the anchovies are so salty you should not need to add salt). Stir in the crème fraîche and allow to boil.

4. Cover and return to the simmering oven for 45 minutes until tender.

5. Just before serving, scatter over the chopped herbs.

tahini and ginger chicken casserole

Serves 6

12 chicken thigh joints
2 tbsp olive oil
1 medium onion
1 clove garlic
1 tbsp plain flour
½ pint (275ml) stock
2 tsp tahini paste
2 balls of stem ginger in syrup
Salt and pepper

Oven:
Aga simmering oven, 250F, 130C, Gas 1

Prepare ahead:
24 hours

Freeze:
Yes

1. Remove the skin from the chicken joints. Peel and chop the onion and crush the garlic.

2. Heat the oil in a casserole pan on the simmering plate and add the chicken, onion and garlic. Transfer the pan to the floor of the roasting oven for 10 minutes to brown.

3. Stir in the flour, then the stock. Add the tahini paste and grate in the ginger, with a tablespoon of syrup. Season, then bring to the boil.

4. Cover and cook in the simmering oven for 45 minutes until cooked through and tender.

5. Serve with celeriac mashed with potatoes and a green vegetable.

sally's spanish chicken

Serves 6

6 chicken breasts
1 tbsp olive oil
1 onion
1 clove garlic
4 oz (110g) chorizo sausage
½ pint (275ml) tomato passata
½ tin pitted black olives
1 tbsp fresh parsley, chopped
1 tsp fresh thyme, chopped

Oven:
Aga simmering oven, 250F,
130C, Gas 1

Prepare ahead:
24 hours

Freeze:
Yes

1. Remove the skin from the chicken joints. Peel and chop the onion and crush the garlic. Slice the chorizo sausage.

2. Heat the oil in a casserole pan on the simmering plate and add the chicken, onion, garlic and chorizo. Transfer the pan to the floor of the roasting oven for 10 minutes to brown.

3. Transfer the pan to the simmering plate and pour on the passata. Bring to the boil and stir in the olives. Cover the pan and transfer to the simmering oven for 45 minutes until tender.

4. Just before serving, stir in the parsley and tyme.

borscht beef casserole

Serves 6

2 lb (900g) stewing beef
1 onion
1 tbsp olive oil
1 oz (25g) butter
1 tbsp ground ginger
2 balls stem ginger
1 tbsp plain flour
½ lb (225g) cooked beetroot
1 orange
1 tbsp sugar
2 cloves garlic
½ pint (275ml) stock or water
Salt and pepper
5 fl oz (150g) soured cream

Oven:
Aga simmering oven, 250F,
130C, Gas 1

Prepare ahead:
24 hours

Freeze:
Yes

1. Cut the meat into 2"/5cm cubes. Peel and slice the onion. Melt the butter and oil in a casserole on the boiling plate and fry the beef and onion until browned – easiest on the floor of the roasting oven. Grate the stem ginger and add. Stir in the flour, ginger and seasoning.

2. Grate the rind of the orange and squeeze the juice into a processor, add the beetroot, garlic and stock. Whizz together, then stir into the casserole dish. Bring to the boil, then cover and cook in the simmering oven for 2 to 2½ hours.

3. Just before serving, pour on the cream and swirl in to the sauce.

pigsty pie

Serves 4

1½ lb (600g) pork
sausagemeat
2 onions
1 can (400g) chopped tomatoes
Salt and pepper
1½ lb (600g) potatoes
¼ pint (150ml) creamy milk
1 oz (25g) butter
Nutmeg
Salt and pepper

Oven:
Aga roasting oven, 400F, 200C,
Gas 6

Prepare ahead:
24 hours

Freeze:
Yes

1. Heat a large, deep frying pan on the boiling plate and add the sausagemeat, breaking it up into chunks. Cook on the floor of the roasting oven for about 10 minutes, stirring from time to time.

2. Peel and chop the onions and add to the pan and cook for a further 10 – 15 minutes, stirring occasionally.

3. Tip the cooked sausagemeat into a sieve, discarding the fat that runs off. Return the meat to the pan. Stir in the tomatoes, season, cover and cook in the simmering oven for about 15 minutes.

4. Meanwhile, cut the potatoes into even sized pieces. Bring to the boil on the boiling plate, then drain, cover and put into the simmering oven to continue cooking for a further 25 minutes until soft. Add the milk and butter to the pan and mash thoroughly, seasoning with salt, pepper and grates of nutmeg.

5. Pile the sausagemeat mixture into an ovenproof dish then add the potato, smoothing the top with a fork.

6. Bake in the centre of the roasting oven for 30 minutes until the top is golden brown.

pork with cider and chickpeas

Serves 4

4 pork chops (or 8 rashers of
pork loin)
1 onion
1 clove garlic
1 tbsp olive oil
1 tin (400g) chickpeas (drained)
1 tbsp chopped fresh thyme
1 tbsp flour
3/4 pint (300ml) dry cider
Salt and pepper

Oven:
Aga simmering oven, 250F,
130C, Gas 1

Prepare ahead:
24 hours

Freeze:
Yes

1. Heat the oil in a heavy pan in the roasting oven for 5 minutes. Add the pork chops. Chop the onion and crush the garlic. Add the onions and garlic to the pan. Cook until sizzling on the boiling plate, then put onto the roasting oven floor for 10 minutes until brown. Stir in the flour.

2. Tip in the chickpeas and thyme, then pour on the cider, stirring all the time; bring to the boil. Season. Once it is boiling, cover and cook in the simmering oven for 30 minutes until tender.

3. Scatter over a little more thyme and serve with mashed potato or rice to absorb the juices.

salmon kedgeree

Serves 4

4 salmon fillet pieces
1 onion
1 clove garlic
2 tbsp olive oil
Grated rind of a lemon
½ pint (275ml) easy-cook rice
Pinch saffron
¾ pint (450ml) stock or water
or water mixed with wine
Salt and pepper
3 oz (75g) frozen peas

Oven:
Aga simmering oven, 250F,
130C, Gas 1

Prepare ahead:
Will keep warm for up to an
hour

Freeze:
Yes

1. Peel and chop the onion, crush the
    garlic. Heat the oil in a large pan on the
    boiling plate. Add onion and garlic, cook
    for 2–3 minutes, then cover and put into
    the simmering oven for 15 minutes to
    soften.

2. Stir in the rice and saffron, then pour over
    the stock. Season, stir well and bring to
    the boil on the boiling plate. Cover and
    put in the simmering oven for 20 minutes.

3. Skin the fish and cut into ½"/1cm cubes.
    Grate over the lemon rind and a little
    black pepper. Stir into the rice, add the
    peas (and optional prawns, mixed
    shellfish etc) and return to the oven for a
    further 5 minutes before serving.

moroccan lamb and lemon pie

Serves 4

1¼ lb (550g) lamb neck fillet
1 lemon
2 onions
2 cloves garlic
1 tsp ground turmeric
1 tbsp olive oil
1 tbsp plain flour
¾ pint (425ml) stock or water

Pastry:
6 oz (175g) self raising flour
½ tsp baking powder
3 oz (75g) suet
2 tbsp chopped fresh coriander
Cold water to bind
Salt and pepper

Oven:
Aga simmering oven, 250F, 130C, Gas 1

Prepare ahead:
Will keep warm for up to an hour

Freeze:
Yes

1. Heat a deep, heavy frying pan on the boiling plate. Cut the lamb into 1" / 2cm cubes and brown in the oil. Set aside and keep warm.

2. Grate the rind of the lemon. Put the onions and garlic into a processor and chop finely. Tip into the pan and when sizzling, cover and cook in the simmering oven until softened – about 10 minutes. Stir in the turmeric, flour, lemon zest, salt and pepper. Put the whole lemon into the processor (no need to wash the bowl!) and whizz, then add to the pan.

3. Pour on the stock and bring to the boil on the boiling plate. Put the browned lamb back into the pan, cover and return to the simmering oven for 45 minutes.

4. To make the pastry: Mix together the flour, baking powder, suet, coriander, salt and pepper. Stir in the water to bind – about 4 tbsp – and mix to a dough. Turn out onto a floured surface and roll into a disc to fit the pan.

5. Lay the pastry over the casserole, cover with tight-fitting lid and put into the simmering oven for 1½ hours. Serve with steamed spinach.

bambi's return

Serves 6

2 lb (900g) venison, diced
3 oz (85g) streaky bacon
4 tbsp olive oil
1 medium onion
2 carrots
2 cloves garlic
1 sprig rosemary
2 tbsp chopped parsley
2 tbsp plain flour
³/₄ pint (450ml) stock
Salt and pepper
2 squares dark chocolate
3 tbsp red wine vinegar
1 tbsp sultanas
1 tbsp candied peel
1 tbsp pine kernels
1 tbsp dark brown sugar

Oven:
Aga simmering oven, 250F,
130C, Gas 1

Prepare ahead:
Will keep warm for up to an
hour

Freeze:
Yes

1. Snip the bacon into small strips and cut
    the venison into ½"/1cm dice. Peel and
    chop the onion, crush the garlic and dice
    the carrots.

2. Heat the oil in a deep casserole pan. Fry
    the venison and bacon on the boiling
    plate until browned all over. Stir in the
    onion, garlic and carrots and cook on the
    simmering plate, stirring most of the time,
    until beginning to soften – about 5
    minutes. Stir in the flour then the stock.
    Return the pan to the boiling plate and
    bring to the boil. Add the rosemary and
    parsley, season well then cover and put
    into the simmering oven to cook gently
    for an hour.

3. Put the remaining ingredients into a bowl
    and set on the back of the Aga to melt
    together.

4. Stir the chocolate mixture into the
    casserole and return to the simmering
    oven for a further 15 minutes. Serve with
    mashed potato or rice and a green
    vegetable.

duck breasts with puy lentils

Serves 4

4 duck breasts
12 oz (340g) puy lentils
½ oz (15g) butter
1 tbsp olive oil
1 lemon
2 tbsp chopped fresh parsley
2 tbsp stock or white wine
Salt and pepper
1 tbsp redcurrant jelly
2 oranges

Oven:
Aga simmering oven; use the grill pan on the floor of the Aga roasting oven

Prepare ahead:
lentils: 24 hours, meat 30 minutes

Freeze:
Yes

1. Wash the lentils and put into a saucepan. Cover with cold water and bring to the boil. Boil hard for 10 minutes, skim off any scum that has floated to the top, then cover and put into the simmering oven for 20 minutes. Drain and keep warm. Melt the butter and olive oil in the warm lentil pan, add the garlic and onion, stirring together. Set onto the simmering plate to cook for a couple of minutes, then cover and cook in the simmering oven for 10 minutes until softened. Grate in the lemon rind and squeeze the juice then add to the pan with the chopped parsley, seasoning and stock. Return the lentils to the pan and mix together. Keep warm in the simmering oven until needed.

2. Put a grill pan into the roasting oven for 10 minutes to heat up.

3. Remove the skin from the duck breasts.

4. Season them well with salt and pepper. Take the hot grill pan from the oven and rub the fat side of a piece of duck skin over the pan. Set it on the boiling plate and add the duck breasts. Put the pan onto the floor of the roasting oven for 5 minutes, then turn the breasts over and return to the oven for a further 10 minutes.

5. Grate the rind from the oranges and squeeze the juice. When the duck breasts are cooked, remove from the pan and set aside to rest for 5 minutes. Pour the orange juice into the grill pan, add the rind and redcurrant jelly and stir until melted. Season well.

6. Cut the breasts into slices. Pile spoonfuls of lentils onto plates, lay the meat on top and pour over the sauce.

tuna loaf

Serves 6

2 x 7 oz (200g) tins tuna
4 eggs
8 oz (225g) cooked peas
1 lemon
1 oz (25g) butter
2 tbsp plain flour
½ pint (275ml) milk
12 Carrs Table Water biscuits
1 tbsp chopped parsley
Salt and pepper

Oven:
Aga 4th runners of roasting
oven or baking oven, 350F,
170C, Gas 4

Prepare ahead:
24 hours

Freeze:
Yes

1. Hard boil the eggs, peel and chop. Put the biscuits into a plastic bag and bash with a rolling pin to crush.

2. Drain the tuna thoroughly and tip into a large bowl. Add the chopped eggs, peas, parsley, seasoning, crushed biscuits and grated rind of half the lemon and a tablespoon of lemon juice. Stir together.

3. Melt the butter in a pan on the simmering plate and stir in the flour then add the milk, and bring to the boil stirring constantly. When it has thickened, season then fold into the tuna mixture.

4. Line a 2lb (1kg) loaf tin with foil and pile the loaf mix into the tin. Smooth the top, cover with foil and bake for 30 minutes.

5. 2 oven Aga: set the tin into the large roasting tin and hang from the lowest runners of the roasting oven, with the cold plain shelf on the 2nd runners, for 25 minutes.

6. 3 and 4 oven Aga: Hang the grid shelf from the lowest runners in the baking oven and set the tin onto it. Cook for about 35 minutes.

7. Take the loaf from the oven and either serve warm with mashed potatoes and a green vegetable or cold with crusty bread and salad.

sticky toffee meringue roulade

Serves 6

4 egg whites
8 oz (225g) caster sugar
2 tbsp sliced almonds
3 tbsp sticky toffee sauce, from a jar
½ pint (275ml) double cream

Oven:
Aga 4th runners of roasting oven with cold shelf over, or centre of baking oven, 375F, 190C, Gas 5

Prepare ahead:
4 hours

Freeze:
No

1. Line the large roasting tin with Bake-O-Glide.

2. Whisk the whites until stiff, then whisk in the sugar, a spoonful at a time.

3. Spread the meringue over the tin, scatter over the almonds, then bake for 15 minutes.

4. Remove from oven and turn out onto a clean tea towel. Leave for 10 minutes to cool.

5. Whip the cream. Spread the toffee sauce over the meringue, then cover with the whipped cream. Roll up and chill, in its towel, for at least an hour.

6. Serve dusted with icing sugar and something fruity to cut the sweetness!

rum and grape pudding

Serves 4

12 oz (340g) seedless black grapes
12 oz (340g) seedless white grapes
4 tbsp dark rum
5 tbsp muscovado sugar
10 fl oz (275ml) Greek yogurt

Prepare ahead:
12 hours

Freeze:
No

1. Wash, dry and halve the grapes. Pile into a pretty bowl.

2. Mix together the yogurt, sugar and rum, stirring until the sugar has dissolved. Fold this into the grapes. Cover and chill until needed.

blackcurrant cake

Serves 6

This also works as a steamed pudding – pile the mixture into a greased 2 pint / 1 litre bowl, put into a deep pan with an inch of water, cover and bring to the boil on the boiling plate, then transfer to the simmering oven for 2½ – 3 hours

4 oz (110g) butter
4 oz (110g) dark muscovado sugar
2 eggs
6 oz (165g) self raising flour
½ tsp baking powder
½ tsp ground cinnamon
6 oz (175g) blackcurrants (fresh, frozen or tinned)
up to 2 tbsp milk or juice from the tin of fruit

Oven:
Aga baking oven, 350F, 170C, Gas 4

Prepare ahead:
keeps warm for up to an hour, also nice cold the next day

Freeze:
Yes

1. Line the base and sides of an 8"/20cm deep cake tin with Bake-O-Glide.

2. Stand the butter beside the Aga to soften.

3. Top and tail the blackcurrants – or defrost of frozen, or drain if canned.

4. Pile the butter, sugar, eggs, flour, baking powder and cinnamon into a processor and whizz until mixed. Add the milk or juice if necessary to make a dropping consistency.

5. Add the blackcurrants and whizz for a second to mix in.

6. Pour into the prepared tin.

7. 2 oven Aga: set the cake tin into the large roasting tin and hang from the lowest runners of the roasting oven, with the cold plain shelf on the 2nd runners, for 25 minutes, then transfer to the simmering oven for a further 30 minutes until cooked.

8. 3 and 4 oven Aga: hang the grid shelf from the lowest runners in the baking oven and set the tin onto it. Cook for about 45 minutes.

9. Turn out and serve with a dollop of crème fraîche.

chocolate roulade

Serves 6 – 8

6 eggs
5 oz (150g) caster sugar
2 oz (55g) cocoa powder

½ pint (275ml) cream
4 oz (110g) white chocolate

Oven:
Aga 4th runners of roasting oven or 3rd runners of baking oven, 350F, 160C, Gas 4

Prepare ahead:
24 hours

Freeze:
Yes

1. Line the large roasting tin with Bake-O-Glide. Put the white chocolate into a bowl and set it on the back of the Aga to melt.

2. Separate 5 of the eggs and whisk the yolks with the sugar, cocoa and one whole egg until pale and fluffy. Whisk the whites until stiff and fold into the mixture.

3. Spread over the tin and bake.

4. 2 oven Aga: hang the tin from the 4th set of runners, with the cold plain shelf on the 2nd runners above, to bake for 15 minutes.

5. 3 and 4 oven Aga: hang the tin from the third runners in the baking oven for 20 minutes.

6. Remove from the oven and tip out onto a clean tea towel. Peel off the Bake-O-Glide and roll up in the tea towel and allow to cool.

7. Whip the cream and fold in the chocolate. Unroll the cake and spread the chocolate mixture over it, then roll up. Chill until needed and serve dusted with icing sugar.

You could also stir some chestnut purée into the cream instead of the white chocolate.

Or cover the finished roulade with whipped cream (perhaps mixed with melted dark chocolate) to make a Christmas chocolate log.

individual raspberry and hazelnut strudels

Serves 4

8 oz (225g) frozen raspberries
4 tbsp caster sugar
4 sheets filo pastry
2 tbsp chopped hazelnuts
1 oz (25g) butter

Oven:
Aga 4th runners of roasting
oven or 3rd runners of baking
oven, 350F, 180C, Gas 4

Prepare ahead:
24 hours

Freeze:
Yes, uncooked. Bake from
frozen for 15-20 minutes

1. Set the butter in a bowl on the back of the Aga to melt.

2. Lay out the sheets of pastry and brush all the edges with butter.

3. Pile 2 oz (55g) raspberries and ½ tbsp hazelnuts onto the centre of each sheet. Add a spoonful of sugar.

4. Fold the pastry into a parcel, brushing with butter to seal and brush the top with butter.

5. Bake for 10–12 minutes, until golden. Serve with crème fraîche.

cherry and sour cream clafoutis

Serves 4 – 6

Large jar (450g) cherries in natural juice
5 fl oz (150ml) soured cream
3½ oz (100g) plain flour
2 eggs
3 oz (75g) soft brown sugar
Couple of drops vanilla essence

To serve:
Icing sugar

Oven:
Aga roasting oven, 400F, 200C, Gas 6

Prepare ahead:
1 hour

Freeze:
No

1. Drain the cherries through a sieve, reserving the juice.

2. Tip them into an 11"/27cm non-stick round baking tin.

3. Mix together all the remaining ingredients, plus 5 fl oz / 150ml of the cherry juice.

4. Pour the batter over the cherries and bake at the top of the roasting oven for 20–25 minutes until puffed up and golden.

5. Serve dusted with icing sugar and a spoonful of crème fraîche.

hot chocolate pudding with white chocolate sauce

Serves 4–6

Steamed puddings are ever popular, especially in the depths of winter!

4 oz (110g) plain chocolate
2 eggs
4 oz (110g) butter
4 oz (110g) soft light brown sugar
6 oz (175g) self-raising flour
1 orange

Sauce:
4 oz (110g) white chocolate
4 tbsp crème fraîche

Oven:
Aga simmering oven, 250F, 130C, Gas 1

Prepare ahead:
24 hours

Freeze:
Yes

1. Set the dark and white chocolates, in different bowls, on the back of the Aga to melt for 20 minutes.

2. Grate the rind of the orange and squeeze the juice into a large bowl. Add the butter, sugar, flour and eggs to the orange rind and juice and mix well. Stir in the chocolate.

3. Pour into a greased 2 pint (1 litre) pudding basin, cover and place in a deep pan filled with about 1"/2cm of water and a slice of lemon (to stop the water discolouring the pan). Cover.

4. Bring to the boil then simmer for 5 minutes before putting into the simmering oven for at least 3 hours.

5. For the sauce, stir the crème fraîche into the melted white chocolate.

6. To serve, turn out onto a plate and hand round the sauce separately.

butterscotch tart

Serves 6

I know; in Agaland we don't bake pastry blind, but in this case it really makes a difference!

7 oz (200g) plain flour
3½ oz (100g) butter
Small can evaporated milk
6 oz (175g) dark muscovado sugar

To finish:
1 tbsp icing sugar

Oven:
Aga roasting oven, 400F, 200C, Gas 6

Prepare ahead:
12 hours

Freeze:
No

1. First make the pastry: whizz the butter and flour in a processor until chopped and mixed, then add tablespoons of water to bind into a dough. Tip onto a floured surface and roll out to line a 10"/25cm flan tin. Chill the pastry.

2. Fill the tin with scrumpled foil and bake for 15 minutes on the floor of the roasting oven.

3. Whilst it is baking, beat together the evaporated milk and sugar – this takes at least 5 minutes – until it is thickened and pale.

4. Take the pastry case from the oven, remove the foil, pour in the filling and return to the oven for 8 minutes until set.

5. Remove from the oven, allow to cool, dust with icing sugar and serve.

pecan and maple pie

Serves 4 – 6

6 oz (175g) plain flour
1 oz (25g) caster sugar
3 oz (75g) butter
2 tbsp cold water

4 oz (110g) pecan nuts
6 tbsp maple syrup
2 oz (50g) butter
3 oz (75g) light brown sugar
3 eggs

Oven:
Aga roasting oven, 400F, 200C,
Gas 6

Prepare ahead:
1 hour

Freeze:
Yes

1. Set the 2oz (50g) butter in a bowl on the back of the Aga to melt.

2. To make the pastry, whizz the flour, caster sugar and 3 oz (75g) butter in a processor. Add sufficient water to bind into a dough. Roll out and line an 8"/20cm flan dish. Chill for at least half an hour.

3. Take the bowl of melted butter and stir in the maple syrup, brown sugar and eggs. Pour into the pastry case.

4. Scatter the pecan nuts over the top then bake on the floor of the roasting oven for 15 – 20 minutes.

5. Serve warm.

You could add a bar (100g) of melted chocolate instead of the maple syrup.

raspberry soufflés

Serves 4

8 oz (225g) raspberries – fresh
or frozen
4 oz (110g) caster sugar
4 egg whites
Butter for greasing the dishes

To finish:
1 tbsp (15g) icing sugar

Oven:
Aga roasting oven, 400F, 200C,
Gas 6

Prepare ahead:
Mix up to an hour beforehand,
but cook at the last minute

Freeze:
No

1. With a piece of kitchen paper and some butter, grease the inside of 4 ramekin dishes.

2. Mash the raspberries with a fork (or push through a sieve if you don't like the pips!).

3. Whisk the egg whites until stiff, then whisk in the sugar, a spoonful at a time, until it is thick and glossy.

4. Fold in the raspberries then pour into the prepared ramekin dishes. Bake for 12–15 minutes until golden and puffed up. Dust with icing sugar and serve at once.

This works well with a jar of cherry compote (Bonne Maman is lovely) for an instant storecupboard pudding.

You could also try using a jar of marmalade instead of the raspberries.

alton cheesecake

Serves 6

2 Mars bars
2 x 7 oz (200g) packs low fat
cream cheese
2 oz (50g) butter
7 oz (200g) pack chocolate
coated ginger nut biscuits

Prepare ahead:
24 hours

Freeze:
Yes

1. Cut the Mars bars into pieces and put into a bowl. Add the cream cheese and set on the back of the Aga to melt.

2. Put the butter into a large bowl on the back of the Aga to melt. Crush the biscuits and stir into the melted butter. Tip the mixture into an 8"/20cm metal flan case. Press the biscuit mix onto the base and up the sides, then refrigerate for an hour to set.

3. Beat the melted Mars bars and cream cheese together and pour into the prepared case. Chill until set, then serve with a fruit coulis or some fresh fruit.

You could substitute caramel-flavoured chocolate for the Mars bars, or try melting some segments of chocolate orange, if you have found one at the bottom of your Christmas stocking.

Use up a handful of the chocolates left in the bottom of a selection box after everyone has eaten their favourites!

chocolate and ginger queen of puddings

Serves 4 – 6

½ loaf brioche
¾ pint (425ml) milk
1 oz (25g) cocoa powder
1 oz (25g) stem ginger + 2 tbsp syrup from ginger jar
3 eggs
Knob of butter
5 oz (130g) caster sugar

Oven:
Aga 4th runners of roasting oven (or centre of baking oven), 375F, 190C, Gas 5

Prepare ahead:
24 hours without meringue

Freeze:
No

1. Cut the brioche loaf into ½"/1cm slices. Use the butter to grease the inside of a 10"/25cm flan dish.

2. Lay the slices of brioche to cover the base of the dish. Heat the milk with the cocoa powder and 3 oz (75g) of the caster sugar and stir until dissolved. Grate in the stem ginger and add the syrup. Mix, then allow to cool.

3. Separate the eggs. Mix the yolks into the chocolatey milk then pour over the brioche. If possible, leave to stand for up to an hour to soak into the bread.

4. <u>2 oven Aga:</u> put the grid shelf onto the floor of the roasting oven and put the dish onto the grid. Put the cold plain shelf over the dish and bake for 20 minutes until set.

5. <u>3 and 4 oven Aga:</u> set the dish on the grid shelf on the 4th runners in the baking oven. Bake for 20 minutes until set.

6. Whisk the egg whites until stiff, then fold in the remaining 2 oz (55g) sugar. Put spoonfuls of the meringue onto the pudding, making sure that it meets the edges of the dish. Return to the oven, still under the plain shelf, for 5–10 minutes until golden. Serve at once.

rhubarb and ginger pudding

Serves 4 – 6

1 lb (450g) rhubarb
3 balls stem ginger
2 tbsp soft brown sugar
6 oz (175g) butter
6 oz (175g) caster sugar
3 eggs
6 oz (175g) self raising flour
1 tsp baking powder
1 tsp ground ginger
1 tbsp chopped almonds

Oven:
Aga 4th runners of roasting or middle of baking oven, 350F, 170C, Gas 4

Prepare ahead:
1 hour

Freeze:
No

1. Butter an 8"/20cm flan dish.

2. Trim and slice the rhubarb into $1/4$"/$1/2$ cm slices. Grate the stem ginger. Mix these with the brown sugar and tip into the greased dish.

3. Pile the butter, caster sugar, eggs, flour and baking powder into a processor and whizz until well mixed. Pour onto the rhubarb mixture and smooth the top.

4 Sprinkle over the ground ginger and almonds.

5. 2 oven Aga: set the dish into the large roasting tin and hang from the lowest runners of the roasting oven, with the cold shelf on the 2nd runners for 25 minutes, then transfer to the simmering oven for a further 30 minutes until set.

6. 3 and 4 oven Aga: hang the grid shelf from the lowest runners in the baking oven and set the dish onto it. Cook for about 45 minutes until set.

If you can't get rhubarb, try some halved plums.

sticky chocolate cake

Serves 6

7 oz (200g) plain chocolate
8 oz (225g) butter
8 oz (225g) soft brown sugar
2 tbsp cocoa powder
5 fl oz (150ml) milk
5 fl oz (150ml) water
2 eggs
12 oz (350g) plain flour
1 tsp baking powder

Oven:
Aga 4th runners of roasting oven 375F, 190C, Gas 5, then simmering oven (or centre of baking oven).

Prepare ahead:
24 hours if to eat cold

Freeze:
Yes, the cake becomes even moister when defrosted!

1. In a deep pan, melt together the butter, chocolate, water, milk and sugar on the simmering plate. Remove from the heat and leave to cool for a few minutes.

2. Line the base and sides of a 9"/23cm deep cake tin with Bake-O-Glide.

3. Beat the eggs into the chocolate mixture, then stir in the flour, cocoa and baking powder.

4. Pour into the prepared tin and bake

5. 2 oven Aga: set the tin into the large roasting tin and hang from the lowest runners of the roasting oven, with the cold shelf on the 2nd runners for 25 minutes, then transfer to the simmering oven for a further 30 minutes until set.

6. 3 and 4 oven Aga: hang the grid shelf from the lowest runners in the baking oven and set the tin onto it. Cook for about 45 minutes until set.

7. Serve warm, with generous dollops of natural yogurt.

christmas cake

This amount will fill an 8"/20cm round or 7"/18cm square cake tin. Double the quantity for a 10"/25cm round or 9"/23cm square tin and double that again for a 12"/30cm round or 11"/28cm square tin, perhaps for a wedding cake.

1½ lb (600g) dried fruit: mixed sultanas, raisins and currants
8 oz (225g) glacé cherries
2 oz (50g) chopped candied peel
8 fl oz (225 ml) ruby port
½ tsp orange oil or the grated rind of an orange
2 oz (50g) ground almonds
6 oz (175g) self raising flour
6 oz (175g) butter
6 oz (175g) dark muscovado sugar
3 eggs
2 tbsp black treacle
1 tsp mixed spice

2 tbsp brandy

3 further tbsp brandy

Redcurrant jelly or apricot jam
About 1lb (500g) almond paste
Icing

Oven:
Aga simmering oven, 250F, 130C, Gas 1

Prepare ahead:
3 months

Freeze:
No need

1. Line the base and sides of an 8"/20cm deep round cake tin with Bake-O-Glide.

2. Wash the fruit and pile into a bowl. Stir in the port and orange oil or rind. Cover and leave to steep for 24 hours, or longer.

3. Mix together the almonds, butter, flour, sugar, eggs, treacle and spice. Fold in the soaked fruit.

4. Pour into the tin and bake in the simmering oven for about 6 to 8 hours – some ovens are faster than others! When a clean skewer inserted into the centre comes out clean, the cake is cooked.

5. Leave to cool, then spoon over 2 tbsp brandy. Leave for about 6 hours to soak, then wrap in greaseproof paper and store in a cool cupboard – not the fridge – for up to 3 months. About once a month, open the package and spoon over a little more brandy. *Do not pierce the cake with a skewer once it is cooked and cooled, the brandy will soak in quite easily without.*

6. About 3 weeks before the cake is needed (ie. at the beginning of December), remove from the paper and brush the cake with melted redcurrant jelly or apricot jam, then cover in almond paste, ice and decorate.

almond paste

8 oz (225g) ground almonds
4 oz (110g) caster sugar
4 oz (110g) icing sugar
½ tsp almond essence
1 egg
Juice of ½ lemon (about 1½ tbsp)

Prepare ahead:
24 hours

Freeze:
No

1. Mix together the almonds and sugars. Beat in the egg, and almond essence then add the lemon, until the mixture forms a pliable paste.

2. Knead the paste until smooth then roll out, using plenty of icing sugar on the board to prevent it from sticking. Roll it out into a circle about 3"/8cm larger than the cake.

3. Set the cake onto a cake board or large flat plate and brush with boiled redcurrant jelly or boiled and sieved apricot jam. Lay the almond paste over the cake and smooth it over the top and down the sides, to form a complete covering.

4. Leave for 24 hours or up to a week to dry out before icing and decorating.

royal icing

1 egg white *or equivalent amount of pasteurised dried egg mixed with water, about 1 fl oz (25ml)*
1 lb (450g) icing sugar
½ tsp liquid glycerine (*to prevent the icing from setting like rock!*)
Few drops of food colouring if required

1. Put the egg white into a large bowl with the glycerine and stir in the icing sugar, a spoonful at a time, until it forms a thick mass. Do not use an electric whisk as that will add too much air and make meringue rather than smooth icing!

2. The icing should be thick, smooth and glossy, but not too thick – it needs to hold its shape when stirred, rather like cement!

3. Using a palate knife, spread the icing over the prepared cake, swirling it into a snow-like pattern, or leaving it smooth.

Smooth Royal icing is easier to apply if you cover it in a couple of thin layers of icing, leaving it to set in between, rather than piling all the icing on at once and then smoothing it.

Add a little colouring and pipe on some Christmassy decorations or words. Alternatively, cut out shapes from coloured fondant icing and stick on with a little Royal icing or, easier still, stick on some plastic Father Christmas type ornaments.

Alternatively, you can buy ready-made fondant icing, which you just roll out and lay over the cake then trim to fit. Or buy a ready rolled pack and just unwrap it and put it on! Brush the cake with cooled boiled water or brandy before putting on the icing to make it stick.

quick mince pies

Makes 24

1 lb (450g) puff pastry
1 egg

Filling:
12 oz (340g) jar mincemeat
(see page 108)

Oven:
Aga roasting oven,
400F, 200C, Gas 6

Prepare ahead:
24 hours, uncooked

Freeze:
Yes, uncooked

1. Roll out the pastry to $1/8$" / 3mm thick and lay onto a 24-hole mini muffin tin. Brush with beaten egg.

2. Put about $2/3$ teaspoon of the mincemeat into each dip, then fold over the remaining pastry and press down the edges to seal with the rolling pin. Flip the tin over to release the pastry, then cut out the pies with a 2"/5cm cutter.

3. Brush with beaten egg, lay onto a baking sheet and bake for 12–15 minutes, until risen and browned. Serve warm, with brandy butter.

christmas mincemeat

Makes about 5 jars

The perfect present for Teacher at Christmas!

8 oz (225g) cooking apples
2 lb (1 kg) packet mixed dried fruit
4 oz (110g) glacé cherries
1 pack (225g) shredded suet (can be vegetarian)
1 lb (450g) dark muscovado sugar
2 tsp mixed spice
1 tsp ground allspice
¼ pint (150ml) brandy
Grated rind and juice of a lemon

Oven:
Aga simmering oven, 250F, 130C, Gas 1

Prepare ahead:
1 month

Freeze:
No need

1. Peel, core and grate the apples. Pile into a bowl with all the other ingredients and mix.

2. Cover and leave overnight for the fruit to absorb the brandy

3. Next day, put into the simmering oven for 2 hours, to melt the suet.

4. Remove from oven, stir well and put into sterilised jars. Seal, label and put in a safe place until Christmas!

christmas drop scones

4 oz (110g) self raising flour
1 oz (25g) caster sugar
1 egg
½ tsp baking powder
¼ pint (150ml) milk
½ tsp mixed spice
1 oz (25g) sultanas

Prepare ahead:
No

Freeze:
No

1. Put all the ingredients except the sultanas into a bowl and whisk together. Stir in the sultanas.

2. Put a sheet of Bake-O-Glide onto the simmering plate.

3. Put spoonfuls of the mixture onto the plate, spaced well apart. When the bubbles rise to the surface – a minute or two – turn the drop scones over and cook the other side for a further minute.

4. Pile them onto a plate (cover with a clean tea towel to keep them soft until needed) and serve with butter.

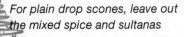

For plain drop scones, leave out the mixed spice and sultanas

sally's fudge biscuits

1 tin (405g) condensed milk
7 oz (200g) butter
4 tbsp golden syrup
1 lb (450g) digestive biscuits
4 oz (110g) plain chocolate

Prepare ahead:
Keep for a week in an airtight
container

Freeze:
Yes

1. Line the small roasting tin with Bake-O-Glide.

2. Break up the chocolate and set the bowl on the back of the Aga to melt.

3. Empty the tin of condensed milk into a pan, add the butter and syrup and slowly bring to the boil on the simmering plate. Cook for 10 minutes until golden.

4. Crush the biscuits and stir into the fudge mixture. Pour into the tin and allow to cool.

5. Spread the melted chocolate over the top of the fudge. Chill until set. Turn out, and cut into 1"/2cm squares and eat.

caroline's olive loaf

9 oz (250g) self raising flour
4 eggs
5 oz (150g) gruyère cheese
5 oz (150g) green olives, sliced
2 thick slices smoked ham
4 fl oz (125ml) white wine
4 fl oz (125ml) sunflower oil

Oven:
Aga 4th runners of roasting
oven, 375F, 190C,
Gas 5

Prepare ahead:
12 hours

Freeze:
Yes

1. Line a 2lb/1kg loaf tin with Bake-O-Glide.

2. Grate the cheese, slice the olives and cut the ham into small cubes.

3. Mix all the ingredients together in a large bowl and pour into the prepared tin. Put onto the grid shelf on the floor of the roasting oven for 40 minutes (you may need the cold plain shelf to protect the top from browning too fast after about 25 minutes).

apple, cheese and walnut loaf

8 oz (225g) self raising flour
1 tsp salt
1 tsp bicarbonate of soda
1 tsp baking powder
1 tsp ground cinnamon
2 oz (55g) caster sugar
4 oz (110g) cheddar cheese
2 oz (50g) walnuts, chopped
1 Bramley cooking apple
3 oz (75g) butter
2 eggs
3 fl oz (75ml) milk

Oven:
Aga 4th runners of roasting
oven or centre of baking oven,
350F, 170C, Gas 4

Prepare ahead:
24 hours

Freeze:
Yes

1. Set the butter in a bowl on the back of
   the Aga to melt.

2. Sift the flour, salt, bicarbonate, baking
   powder, cinnamon and sugar into a large
   bowl. Grate the cheese and add, with the
   chopped walnuts.

3. Peel, core and grate the apple and add
   to the bowl. Mix together.

4. Add the eggs and milk to the melted
   butter and pour onto the dry ingredients.
   Mix together thoroughly.

5. Line a 2lb/1kg loaf tin with foil and pour
   the mixture into it.

6. 2 oven Aga: set the loaf tin into the large
   roasting tin and hang from the 4th
   runners in the roasting oven, with the
   cold plain shelf on the 2nd runners. Bake
   for 30 minutes, then transfer the roasting
   tin to the simmering oven for 20 minutes
   to finish cooking.

7. 3 and 4 oven Aga: set the grid shelf on
   the floor of the baking oven and put the
   loaf tin onto it. Cook for 45 minutes until
   risen and browned.

8. The cake is cooked when a skewer
   pushed into the middle comes out clean.

9. Turn onto a cooling rack and once cool,
   slice and serve, buttered.

stilton biscuits

4 oz (110g) wholemeal plain flour
4 oz (110g) Stilton cheese
4 oz (110g) butter
1/4 tsp mustard powder
1 tbsp cold water
1 egg

Oven:
Aga 4th runners of roasting oven, 400F, 200C,
Gas 6

Prepare ahead:
eat cold up to 48 hours later

Freeze:
Yes

1. Line the cold plain shelf with Bake-O-Glide.
2. Put the flour, cheese, butter and mustard into a processor and whizz. Add a little of the water and whizz again until it comes together as a dough.
3. Tip onto a floured surface and knead for a minute, then roll out to 1/4"/1/2cm thickness. Brush with beaten egg and cut into triangles.
4. Lay the biscuits onto the shelf and hang from the bottom set of runners in the roasting oven for 10 minutes until puffed up and golden.
5. Serve warm.

mrs m's fudge

1 tin condensed milk
4 oz (110g) butter
2 lb (1kg) granulated sugar
1 tbsp vanilla essence
1/4 pint (150ml) water

Prepare ahead:
Lasts up to a week, allegedly!

Freeze:
No

1. Line the small roasting tin with Bake-O-Glide.
2. Put the water into a heavy based pan and set on the simmering plate. Add the butter, sugar and condensed milk. Gradually heat until everything is melted, then boil, stirring all the time, for 10 minutes.
3. Remove from the heat and stir in the vanilla.
4. Tip the fudge into the tin and allow to cool, scoring into squares before it has set completely.

pecan and maple scones

9 oz (250g) self raising flour
1 tsp baking powder
2 oz (55g) butter
1 egg
4 tbsp maple syrup
4 tbsp milk
2 oz (55g) pecan nuts

Oven:
Aga roasting oven, 400F, 200C,
Gas 6

Prepare ahead: one hour

Freeze:
Yes, reheat for a minute before
eating

1. Line the cold plain shelf with Bake-O-Glide.

2. Put all the ingredients into a processor and whizz briefly until mixed. Turn out onto a floured board and pat or roll out to 1/2" /1cm thick.

3. Using a 2"/5cm cutter, cut out scones and place on the Bake-O-Glide. Re-roll the trimmings to make more scones. Brush with milk and hang from the third set of runners. Bake for 10–12 minutes until risen and golden.

4. Serve with crème fraîche and maple syrup.

fudge blondies

3 eggs
6 oz (175g) light brown sugar
6 oz (175g) butter
8 oz (225g) self raising flour
1 tsp baking powder
2 tbsp milk
3 1/2 oz (100g) pack white
chocolate drops

Oven:
Aga 4th runners of roasting
oven or centre of baking oven,
375F, 190C, Gas 5

Prepare ahead:
Keeps for 3 days

Freeze:
Yes

1. Line the small roasting tin with Bake-O-Glide. Set the butter beside the Aga to soften for a few minutes.

2. Beat the eggs, sugar, butter, flour, baking powder and milk together, then fold in the white chocolate drops.

3. Pour into the tin and smooth the top.

4. Bake for 25–30 minutes (you may need to slide the cold plain shelf onto the runners above the cake after about 20 minutes to protect the top from browning too fast).

apricot and citrus traybake

Traybakes are all the rage, and it is easy to see why – cut into slices or squares, they can be made to go a long way!

4 oz (110g) ready to eat, no need to soak, dried apricots
2 oz (55g) dried mixed citrus peel
3 eggs
6 oz (175g) caster sugar
6 oz (175g) butter
8 oz (225g) self raising flour
1 tsp baking powder
2 tbsp orange juice

2 tbsp Demerara sugar

Oven:
Aga bottom runners of roasting oven or centre of baking oven, 375F, 190C, Gas 5

Prepare ahead:
Keeps for 3 days

Freeze:
Yes

1. Line the small roasting tin with Bake-O-Glide. Set the butter beside the Aga to soften for a few minutes.

2. Chop the apricots into small pieces.

3. Beat the eggs, sugar, butter, flour, baking powder and orange juice together, then fold in the apricots and peel.

4. Pour into the tin, smooth the top and sprinkle over the Demerara sugar.

5. <u>2 oven Aga:</u> set the tin into the large roasting tin and hang from the 4th runners in the roasting oven, with the cold plain shelf on the 2nd runners. Bake for 25 minutes, then transfer the roasting tin to the simmering oven for 15 minutes to finish cooking.

6. <u>3 and 4 oven Aga:</u> set the grid shelf on the floor of the baking oven and put the tin onto it. Cook for 30 minutes until risen and browned.

7. Cool on a rack and cut into squares or fingers.

granny's shortbread

Makes 24 squares

Made by Granny every week and positively inhaled by the grandchildren at weekends. My nephew was once overheard telling his friend, 'have some of this, it's all they have here'. With shortbread, simple really is best!

12 oz (340g) plain flour
8 oz (225g) butter, cut up
4 oz (110g) caster sugar

Oven:
Aga 4th runners of roasting oven or centre of baking oven, 375F, 190C, Gas 5

Prepare ahead:
3 days

Freeze:
Yes

1. Put the flour into a bowl and rub in the butter, then stir in the sugar. Alternatively, pile everything into a processor and whizz until mixed and like breadcrumbs.

2. Line the small roasting tin with Bake-O-Glide and pour in the mixture. Press down evenly – use the base of a tumbler for speed! – then hang from the lowest set of runners for 15–20 minutes until pale golden. (You may need to slide in the cold plain shelf after 10 minutes to prevent it from browning too fast.)

3. Cool in the tin then turn out and cut into 24 squares.

millionaire's shortbread

Use the shortbread as a base, then spread over 4 tbsp toffee sauce from a jar. Melt 4 oz (110g) plain chocolate and spread over the sauce. Chill until set, then cut up and serve.

flavoured oil and vinegar

2 pints (1 litre) olive oil – not best quality
Herbs to flavour: basil, rosemary, thyme, lavender

2 pints white wine vinegar
Herbs to flavour: tarragon, marjoram, basil

1. Bruise the herbs slightly and put into a large jar. Warm the oil or vinegar then pour over herbs and leave to absorb the flavours for at least a week.

2. Pour into pretty bottles and add sprigs of the chosen herb. Label, decorate and either give as presents or keep for yourself!

crabapple jelly

Makes about 6 lbs

3lbs (1.5kg) crabapples (or apples)
3 pints (1.5litres) water
3lbs (1.5kg) granulated sugar, approx

1. Pile the crabapples into a preserving pan and add the water. Bring to the boil on the boiling plate, cover and put into the simmering oven for about 30 minutes, until the fruit is soft.

2. Allow to cool and pour into a jelly bag. Leave to drip through the bag for at least 12 hours or overnight.

3. Next day, measure the juice into a clean pan and for each pint of liquid, allow a pound of sugar. Boil hard for about 15 minutes, until setting point has been reached. Cool for a few minutes, then pour into sterilised jars and seal.

crabapple and sloe jelly

You can add half a pound of sloes to the crabapples as they boil, for an interesting change. This makes a beautiful, sharp ruby-red jelly. Delicious with game!

crabapple and lavender jelly

Add a large handful of lavender flowers to the crabapples as they simmer. Put a sprig of lavender in each jar just before sealing.

turkish delight

1 lb (450g) caster sugar
1 oz (25g) gelatine
½ pint (330ml) water
1 tsp rosewater
Pink food colouring (optional)
Icing sugar to finish

Oven:
Floor of Aga roasting oven

Prepare ahead:
2 weeks in the fridge

Freeze:
No

1. Pour the water into a heavy based pan,
    and add the sugar and sprinkle on the
    gelatine. Allow to stand for a minute, then
    move to the simmering plate to dissolve
    the sugar and gelatine in the water. Bring
    to the boil and transfer to the floor of the
    roasting oven for 20 minutes, without a
    lid.

2. Take out of the oven and test the delight
    to see if it is ready: dip a wooden spoon
    into it, allow to cool for a minute, then dip
    your fingers into the spoonful. When you
    pull your fingers apart, the delight should
    not form a 'string'. Add the rosewater
    and a few drops of food colouring.

3. Line a 6"/15cm cake tin with Bake-O-
    Glide and pour in the hot mixture. Leave
    to cool and set, then turn out and cut
    into ½"/1cm squares. Toss in a bowl of
    icing sugar then put into a box and wrap.

chocolate truffles

4 oz (110g) plain chocolate
2 oz (55g) unsalted butter
2 egg yolks
Grated rind of an orange
1 tbsp orange juice
3 oz (85g) ground almonds

Cocoa powder to finish

Prepare ahead:
4 days in fridge

Freeze:
Yes

1. Set the chocolate and butter in a bowl onto the back of the Aga to melt for 20 minutes.

2. Stir in the orange rind and juice, egg yolks and ground almonds. Put into the fridge to set and once it is cold, roll into balls and coat in cocoa powder.

3. Arrange in a box, each truffle in a small paper case.

turkey and pepper fricassée

1 lb (450g) cooked turkey, cut into ½"/1cm cubes
1 oz (25g) butter
1 oz (25g) plain flour
1 pint (550ml) turkey stock
1 tin (100g) pimentos
¼ pint (150ml) double cream
2 tbsp fresh breadcrumbs
1 oz (25g) grated cheese

Oven:
Aga roasting oven, 400F, 200C, Gas 6

1. Melt the butter in a heavy-based pan, stir in plain flour, cook on the simmering plate for a minute then stir in the turkey stock. Transfer to the boiling plate and bring to the boil, stirring continually.

2. Open the tin of pimentos, drain and chop roughly. Add to the sauce, together with the cream. Season and stir in the cubed cooked turkey. Pile into an oven proof dish, top with the breadcrumbs and cheese. Hang the grid shelf from the lowest set of runners in the roasting oven and bake for ½ hour until golden.

devilled turkey chunks

1 tbsp tomato ketchup
1 tbsp marmalade
1 tbsp vinegar
1 tbsp honey
1 tbsp chutney
2 lb cooked turkey meat, cut into fairly large chunks

Oven:
Aga roasting oven, 400F, 200C, Gas 6

1. Line a roasting tin with Bake-O-Glide.

2. Mix together all the sauces. Smear over the chunks of turkey meat. Put the meat into the tin and hang from the third set of runners in the roasting oven.

3. Cook for 20 minutes until heated through and bubbling.

turkey hash

Leftover turkey, sausages, bacon rolls, sprouts, roast potatoes, vegetables.
Leftover bread sauce
1 oz (25g) butter

1. Chop the meat etc roughly and stir in the bread sauce. Melt the butter in a frying pan and pile in the ingredients. Season well and press down into the pan.

2. Cook on the floor of the roasting oven for about 10 minutes. Flip over (using a plate) and cook on the other side for a further 10 minutes. Serve cut into wedges, with cranberry sauce.

At last the turkey is finished, and you can make stock to use as a base for soups, for cooking rice or for casseroles.

turkey stock

Makes 4 pints / 2 litres

Turkey carcass once the meat has all been removed
2 onions
2 carrots
2 sticks celery
Sprig parsley
2 bay leaves
4 pints (2 litres) water

Oven:
Aga simmering oven, 250F, 130C, Gas 1

Freeze:
Yes

1. Put the turkey bones into a large pan with the water. Cut up the onions, carrots and celery – no need to peel!

2. Bring to the boil on the boiling plate then transfer to the simmering oven and leave for at least an hour, or overnight.

3. Next day, remove from the oven, strain off the bones and vegetables and allow to cool, then refrigerate.

4. When chilled, skim off any fat on the top, then freeze in small batches.

fried christmas pudding

Leftover Christmas pudding
2 tbsp brandy butter

1. Cut the pudding into slices.
2. Melt the brandy butter in a heavy based pan on the simmering plate, then add the slices of pudding. Fry gently, turning once, until the brandy butter caramelises into a delicious goo.

christmas pudding ice cream

Leftover Christmas pudding
1 tub best quality vanilla ice cream

1. Soften the tub of vanilla ice cream at room temperature for half an hour.
2. Crumble some leftover Christmas pudding into the ice cream, mix well and re-freeze for a couple of hours before serving.

(Although, in fact, it appears that there are fourteen days between Christmas Eve and Twelfth Night!)

Christmas Eve

Lunch	**Tea**	**Supper**
Smoked cod soufflé Fresh bread and butter Mixed green salad	Christmas drop scones	Sweet pepper pots Bambi's Return Aga Rice Lemon cabbage Chocolate roulade

Christmas Day

Lunch/Supper	**Tea**	**Supper/Lunch**
The Christmas Feast!	Christmas cake	Smoked salmon and brown bread

Boxing Day

Lunch/Supper	**Tea**	**Supper/Lunch**
Cold turkey sandwiches Mince pies	Fudge biscuits Christmas cake	Smoked trout salad Leek and Yum pie Mixed green salad Christmas pudding fried in brandy butter

December 27th

Lunch/Supper	**Tea**	**Supper/Lunch**
Toasted cheese and turkey sandwiches Fresh fruit and cheese	Shortbread Christmas cake	Shirley's mushrooms Pork with cider and chickpeas Buttered noodles Mixed salad Rum and grape pudding

December 28th

Lunch	**Tea**	**Supper**
Avocado & coconut soup	Blackcurrant cake	Pigsty pie
Caroline's olive loaf		Braised red cabbage
		Cherry and sour cream clafoutis

December 29th

Lunch	**Tea**	**Supper**
Somerset rarebit	Christmas cake	Spinach and three cheese strudel
Tomato salad		Spiced pheasant breasts
		Fanned potatoes
		Roasted sprouts with chestnuts & bacon
		Pecan and maple pie

December 30th

Lunch	**Tea**	**Supper**
Not quite ratatouille	Pecan and maple scones	Turkey hash
Stilton biscuits		Baked potatoes
		Leeks in Daisy's sauce
		Blackcurrant cake as a steamed pudding

New Year's Eve

Lunch	**Tea**	**Supper**
Turkey soup	Apricot and citrus traybake	Selection of canapés
Apple, cheese and walnut loaf		Borscht beef casserole
		Aga rice
		Orange and honey glazed carrots
		Alton cheesecake

New Year's Day

Lunch	**Tea**	**Supper**
Spring onion & watercress tart	Fudge blondies	Fresh tomato soup
Tomato salad		Slow baked
		marmalade gammon
		Hampshire sauce
		Mashed potatoes
		Lemon cabbage
		Chocolate Christmas
		pudding

January 2nd

Lunch	**Tea**	**Supper**
Pear, proscuitto & parmesan salad	Shortbread	Cod with tomato crust
Bread and butter		Fanned potatoes
		Souffléd cauliflower
		cheese
		Sticky toffee
		meringue roulade

January 3rd

Lunch	**Tea**	**Supper**
Pasta with spinach and red peppers	Drop scones	Chicken thighs with anchovies & white wine
Salad		Celeriac & chestnut mash
		Green salad
		Chocolate and ginger
		Queen of puddings

January 4th

Lunch	**Tea**	**Supper**
Tuna loaf	Mince pies	Glazed venison steaks
Salad		Stilton mash
		Mixed salad
		Raspberry soufflés

January 5th

Lunch	**Tea**	**Supper**
Aubergine gratin	Plain scones	Salmon kedgeree
Green salad		Peas
		Butterscotch tart

Twelfth Night

Lunch	**Tea**	**Supper**
Creamy onion soup	Hot buttered toast	Chicken and
Olive loaf	Millionaire's	mangetout
	shortbread	stir fry
		Noodles
		Hot chocolate
		pudding
		with white chocolate
		sauce

January 7th

Fly to the West Indies for a holiday.